JESUS HEALS

YOUR SICKNESS

TODAY!

GUILLERMO MALDONADO

Our Mission

Called to bring the supernatural power of God to this generation.

Jesus Heals Your Sickness Today

978-1-59272-337-9

Edition January 2018

Project Director: Andres Brizuela
Editor: Jose M Anhuaman
Translation: Adriana Cardona
Cover Design: Jessie Morales

Published by:
King Jesus International Ministry - ERJ Publicaciones
14100 SW 144 Ave. Miami, FL 33186
Tel: (305) 382-3171 - Fax: (305) 675-5770

Category: Healing

Printed in the United States of America

I dedicate this book to the Person that taught me how to walk in faith, to cross line after line and obstacle after obstacle, and whose example in life has been a challenge for me: Jesus of Nazareth. I thank You, my dear Friend, for living, dying, and resurrecting so that we could know the Father and receive our inheritance as God's children. Thank You for surrendering Your life for us in order to give us health and redemption.

FROM THE DESK OF

ORAL ROBERTS

Dear Brother Maldonado:

I love your new book <u>Jesus Heals Your Sickness Today</u>.

This book brings healing to my physical body. It is written with people like me in mind.

I love a writer who is close enough to God's calling in their life who can have confidence to heal the sick and humbly say "I can bring healing to you RIGHT NOW." That is what Jesus said, "Heal the Sick." For our need is NOW.

Thank you for writing this living book on healing in the NOW—THE RIGHT NOW of my life. I feel God touching my body as I read this book. Dr. Maldonado is a very close friend of ORU, the Roberts family, and of me.

I love you dearly,

Oral Roberts

INDEX

INDEX

INTRODUCTION

INTRODUCTION

*M*any years have gone by since I began to be used in the same ministry as the one Jesus walked in while He was on the Earth: to guide man to repentance, and to preach, teach, heal the sick, and cast out demons. During this time, I have had the privilege to witness God's supernatural power, and have admired how He touches and changes the lives of countless people. I have also been able to observe that many people desire to know God, to serve Him and receive His blessings, while others remain planted in the valley of doubt, without knowing His will, without access to the inheritance reserved for His children; and in many cases, without believing that He has the power to perform miracles.

For its part, medical science continues its search for solutions to the physical, mental, and spiritual sicknesses that oppress the world's population. Without a doubt, they have made many advances, but they are far from eradicating diseases from the face of the Earth. It has barely been able to annul some, lessen others, and fight certain symptoms of the worst ones. Yet, the statistical increase of death by AIDS, Cancer, Leukemia, A1-H1 flu, and others demonstrate that we continue to need help from God.

Jesus' sacrifice on the Cross was not just enough to forgive all sins, from all men, from all corners of the Earth, from the beginning to the end of humanity. Rather, as the Bible establishes, by His stripes we are "already" healed. He is the Doctor of doctors, for while He was on Earth, no sick person that sought in Him their healing ever returned home without it. Jesus healed all the sick, delivered all those oppressed by the devil, and paid the price for the salvation of all humanity. We have a Testament with more than 30,000 promises that assure us that absolutely all of our, physical, spiritual, mental, and emotional needs are covered by Him.

My purpose in writing this book is to reveal to you, my dear reader, how to reclaim the inheritance that is rightfully yours. In its pages, you will find the meaning of many promises, as well as a spiritual map to grant you access to them. Just like there are ways to receive a miracle from God, there is also a method to keep it, and even one to lose it if we do not behave properly. God's healing is not magic; rather, it is a miracle, a wondrous act, one which includes conditions to be met and requires a grateful heart. Every miracle begins with a seed sown in the heart of a man or a woman. Every miracle described in this book, as well as the way each was produced, is founded on the Word of God, and backed up by testimonies gathered from the thousands of healings I have seen throughout the length of my ministry.

Dear reader, I invite you to enter the reading of this book with a great expectation, for I know that God will perform great miracles though it, because He has promised me so. He longs for His people to come out of ignorance in regards to sickness, and to know His power and desire to heal them.

God wants to, God can, and God is ready to do so ... are you ready to receive it...? Remember that, *"All things are possible to him who believes."*

CHAPTER I

GOD'S WILL IS TO HEAL

S adly, many people are bedridden in clinics or at home suffering with illnesses that they never expected to have. Today, we hear of new epidemics or outbreaks that may be unknown to many, including those of us who are well-informed. We know of children who suffer from previously unheard-of illnesses that cause irreversible damages. We hear of people whose lives end before medical science can accurately diagnose their illnesses; of cruel health professionals who dare meddle with human pain and suffering, seeking only personal gain. Knowing this leads us to meditate on God's will for mankind. The world needs to know what God has to say on this matter.

Throughout these pages, we will discover what God wants to reveal to us. To begin, it is imperative for us to discover and understand His true, divine will. We need to know if God truly has the power to heal and how we can receive healing. In other words, "Is it God's will to heal the sick?" Until we get the answer and receive the conviction of His desire to heal us, we will not be healed; for no one can claim what God wants to give them if they do not know what that is. At times, some believers take too long resolving this matter and establishing a solid, personal relationship with God's healing power. In most cases, when healing is not received or when it is received but not retained, the basic problem is doubt with respect to God's will.

Is it God's will to heal? Is it God's will to heal everyone or only a select few? Is it possible that sometimes it is God's will for sickness to affect us? Many denominations commonly teach that miracles and healing belong to the apostles' era, and that it ended when the last one died; hence, God no longer heals. This practice has submerged the people into an abyss of ignorance, making them susceptible to sickness. I have ministered healing in churches where over 50% of the people were continually sick; this, because its ministers would teach that certain illnesses were God-given in order to prove their faith.

I do not want to give deep theological explanations on this matter in order to prove a point; rather, let us use common sense. Suppose we say the sickness we suffer from is God's will for our life. In other words, that it is a blessing He gave us to prove our faith and make us more humble. If this were true, the next logical step to take would not be to rid ourselves of the blessing. Therefore, going to the doctor would be the wrong decision because then we would be involving the doctor to fight against God's will for our life. If the illness in our body is part of God's divine plan for our life, why go to the doctor? Why take prescription medication? That reasoning does not make sense. The problem is that people use common sense for other things, but when they enter the church, common sense goes out the door.

> If it were God's will for us to be sick,
> then it is a sin to seek healing.

Four ways in which God reveals His will with respect to healing:

1. It is God's nature to heal.

...And said, 'If you diligently heed the voice of the LORD your God and do what is right in His sight, give ear to His

commandments and keep all His statutes, I will put none of
the diseases on you which I have brought on the Egyptians;
for I am the LORD who heals you.' **EXODUS 15:26**

In Hebrew, the word for healer is *rapha*, meaning
physician or doctor. In Modern Hebrew, the same word
is used in reference to doctors. In light of this, it is safe to
accept that God is saying, "I am your doctor." He reveals
Himself as *the* doctor to His people—that is His nature.
The phrase, "I am", which is in the continuous present
tense, is God's proper name, meaning, "I am the Lord
that is continually healing you." This means that He is
continually healing you and me. This revelation was not
given to the Israelite people because they were looking
for it, but rather, because it was God's pleasure to give it
to them. It was His initiative to share it with His people.
The Lord declares, "I am Jehovah, your doctor, and I will
continue to heal you if you keep certain conditions." The
most important condition is to hear His voice. Verse 26
begins by saying, *"If you diligently heed the voice of the*
LORD your God..." In Hebrew it reads, *"If you hear, hearing*
Jehovah's voice," meaning to hear with both ears. Many
people hear God's voice with their right ear and Satan's
voice with their left. This produces confusion. Now let me
ask, "What are we supposed to hear?" We must hear that
the Lord is our continuous healer and that it is His will to
heal our body. Therefore, receive what belongs to you!
Not because you earned it but by His grace.

> The great secret to receiving your healing
> is to hear by hearing with both ears;
> then, God will be your doctor.

Has God changed since the beginning of time?

For I am the LORD, I do not change; therefore you are not consumed, O sons of Jacob. **MALACHI 3:6**

God never changes. He is always the same. He is our doctor. Therefore, we can seek Him for our healing and receive it.

Every good gift and every perfect gift is from above, and comes down from the Father of lights, with whom there is no variation or shadow of turning. **JAMES 1:17**

In the New Testament, God confirms, once more, that His nature never varies. He continues to be our doctor. We change, but He never changes. If He healed yesterday, He will heal today and tomorrow.

2. The will of God is revealed through Jesus.

...How God anointed Jesus of Nazareth with the Holy Spirit and with power, who went about doing good and healing all who were oppressed by the devil, for God was with Him. **ACTS 10:38**

This is the clearest conclusion of Jesus' ministry, spoken by the Apostle Peter in Cornelius' house. Note that the complete Deity is together in the healing ministry: Father, Son, and Holy Spirit. The participation of each is evident. It is also as clear as day that healing comes from God and sickness from the devil, and that the Father and the Holy Spirit provide healing to humanity through Jesus. No-where in Scripture do we find that Jesus refused to heal anyone seeking healing. He never said, "This sickness is my Father's will for your life; there is a reason why you are sick." Or "This sickness is too serious for Me to heal." He never spoke the words, "This disease is hard to heal because you have suffered with it for too long." Nor did He ever say, "This sickness is incurable." In fact, everyone who approached Jesus was healed. Jesus said:

For I have come down from heaven, not to do My own will, but the will of Him who sent Me. John 6:38

Then He concluded with:

Jesus said to him, 'Have I been with you so long, and yet you have not known Me, Philip? He who has seen Me has seen the Father; so how can you say, Show us the Father?'
JOHN 14:9

When we see Jesus, we also see the Father in action. In the Son's healing ministry, we see the Father working in cooperation with the Holy Spirit. The three are united to heal mankind. Millions of people are sick, right now, because they ignore this truth. Are you one of them? When Jesus came to Earth, He healed everyone who believed in Him.

Testimony: Lupe was in the last stage of breast cancer when she came to our church, and so she was very ill. She had undergone chemotherapy and had lost all of her hair. The doctors only gave her a 10% chance of recovery. Although her breast was removed, the cancer continued. She believed in God and sought His presence, more so after learning from a message I preached saying that we must have intimacy with the Holy Spirit. It was during that time of intimacy that the Holy Spirit revealed to her

19

that she would be healed. Today she is cancer-free; it has completely disappeared.

3. The divine will to heal is revealed in the work at the Cross.

The work done by the Father at the Cross, through Jesus' death, is cited in the Old and New Testament:

He is despised and rejected by men, a Man of sorrows and acquainted with grief. And we hid, as it were, our faces from Him; He was despised, and we did not esteem Him. Surely He has borne our griefs and carried our sorrows; yet we esteemed Him stricken, smitten by God, and afflicted. But He was wounded for our transgressions, He was bruised for our iniquities; the chastisement for our peace was upon Him, and by His stripes we are healed. **ISAIAH 53:3-5**

At the Cross, Jesus provided for us spiritually in addition to paying the wages of our rebellion, sin, and transgression. He carried our sickness and physical pain. By His stripes we are healed. In other words, His redeeming work at the Cross reaches every aspect of our lives: emotional, physical, and mental.

What Divine Interchange Took Place at the Cross?

The work of the Cross is perfect in every aspect. The essence of His sacrifice is the divine interchange, ordained by God, through which Jesus took our place and we took His. He took upon Himself our inheritance of death to give us His inheritance of life. At the Cross, Jesus provided for our every need: spiritual, emotional, and physical, for now and for eternity. Following is a list of aspects regarding the divine interchange that took place at the Cross:

- Jesus was punished so that we could be forgiven
- Jesus was wounded so that we could be healed
- Jesus became sin because of our wickedness so we could be made just by His justice
- Jesus died the death we should have suffered so we could receive His life
- Jesus became a curse, so we could receive blessings
- Jesus took our poverty, so we could share in His abundance
- Jesus took our shame, so we could share in His glory
- Jesus accepted our rejection, so we could be accepted by Him

4. God's will is revealed by the written Word and the Holy Spirit.

My son, give attention to my words; incline your ear to my sayings. Do not let them depart from your eyes; keep them in the midst of your heart; for they are life to those who find them, and health to all their flesh. **PROVERBS 4:20-22**

From Genesis to Revelation, we read over and over again the confirmation of what has always been God's will: to heal His people. The verse we just read says that if we confess His Word, if we obey it and keep it in our heart, it becomes medicine to our body. I know many people who were suffering with different ailments. They began listening to messages regarding healing, Continuously. Hearing that word caused them to believe, which lead to their declaration of faith, even while some were still in the hospital. Many were healed. For them—and for us—the Word of God became medicine to their bones. I suggest you do the same. If you are sick, begin to hear God's Word

21

on healing. Listen to healing messages at home, in your car, and everywhere else you go. Meditate and believe on what God says concerning healing, and you will be another person healed by the power of His Word.

How Curses Entered Mankind

How did curses enter mankind? Let us read a few statistics concerning sickness, how it is invading the Earth, and how doctors find it impossible to deal with it; hence, the importance of believing in the supernatural power of God to destroy it and heal us.

HIV: The World Health Organization estimates that 1,018 out of 100,000 people around the globe have HIV. This means there are over 70 million people around the world infected with the disease.

MAIN CAUSE OF DEATH: A third of all deaths around the world are caused by HIV, malaria, tuberculosis, and other contagious diseases. Africa, the southeastern countries in Asia, and the Arabian Peninsula head the list of countries with the most deaths due to these diseases.

INFANT DEATH: 58 out of 1,000 children under the age of five do not survive to adulthood, and a third of these deaths are caused by malnutrition. The main causes of death among children less than five years of age are due to: neonatal complications (43.2%), pneumonia (11.3%), diarrhea (9.3%), lesions (5.0%), malaria (4.0%), HIV (3.3%), measles (1.3%), and other causes (22.6%). African countries register the greatest levels of infant death on record.

CANCER: No country or continent is free from this ailment. The average number of deaths registered worldwide for cancer is 131 for every 100,000. Mongolia, Bolivia, Hungary, Granada, Sierra Leona, Poland, the Czech Republic, and Peru register the highest number of deaths. Cancer attacks the same way in Asia, Latin America, Europe, and Africa, regardless of whether the country is developed or not. The United States registers 134 deaths per 100,000 people due to cancer. This means that close to half a million people will die per year due to this sickness; and this is not to be confused with the number of people who are currently suffering with one type of cancer or another and whose condition is not punctually proportioned by the World Health Organization [1].

The curse of sickness came upon mankind when the first man, Adam, chose to separate himself from God's government to become independent. When this happened, Satan was able to govern over him. The grave consequence that resulted was the triplication of the curse upon mankind. The curse received at the Garden of Eden was handed down to all men, from generation to generation. You might be asking yourself right now, "What is the triple curse?" The triple curse is sin, poverty, and sickness. Yes, sickness! Adam's sin paved the way for the curse of sickness, the subject covered by this book. We will learn how we can be free from this curse and how to retain our healing through Jesus' sacrifice and the power He conquered at the Cross.

What is the Definition of Sickness?

Sickness is the demonic perversion of God's absolute, perfect, and creative work. His Word is clear when it affirms that Jesus redeemed us from the curse of sickness:

---

1   World-wide statistics 2009 from the World Health Organization: www.who.int

Christ has redeemed us from the curse of the law, having become a curse for us, for it is written, 'Cursed is everyone who hangs on a tree.' **GALATIANS 3:13**

If Satan's goal is to corrupt, steal, kill, and destroy, then we can say that when a sick person receives healing, a work of the devil is being destroyed. There is a diabolic and obvious intelligence in many sicknesses such as cancer, tuberculosis, AIDS, multiple sclerosis, etc., called a wicked or evil spirit.

What Is the Origin of Sickness?

According to Scripture, every sickness is directly related with demonic activity. Jesus treated the sick and those tormented by evil spirits the same way. He used the same words to heal and to rebuke the spirits.

Testimony: While ministering in a crusade, I heard the Holy Spirit clearly say the name, Esperanza. I called out the name and a woman responded. She went forward, taking the place of her 73-year-old mother-in-law, also called Esperanza, who was hospitalized at the time and diagnosed with brain cancer. The daughter-in-law wanted a handkerchief to give to her mother-in-law. I prayed for Esperanza and rebuked the spirit of death over her life. God healed her in the hospital. The demonic spirit of sickness had to let her go, and she was completely healed.

Why Did Jesus Come?

He who sins is of the devil, for the devil has sinned from the beginning. For this purpose the Son of God was manifested, that He might destroy the works of the devil. **1 JOHN 3:8**

This verse makes it clear that people suffering with epilepsy, cancer, AIDS, deafness, migraines, and other ailments are tormented by evil spirits through sickness.

■ Matthew confirms it:

When evening had come, they brought to Him many who were demon-possessed. And He cast out the spirits with a word, and healed all who were sick, that it might be fulfilled which was spoken by Isaiah the prophet, saying: 'He Himself took our infirmities and bore our sicknesses.' **MATTHEW 8:16, 17**

Matthew was an Orthodox Levy with knowledge on Hebraic culture; a pure Jew who, inspired by the Holy Spirit, cited the book of Isaiah and showed how Jesus healed the sick.

■ Peter also corroborates this:

...Who Himself bore our sins in His own body on the tree, that we, having died to sins, might live for righteousness— by whose stripes you were healed. **1 PETER 2:24**

Peter combines the spiritual side—being free from sin— with God's justice and physical healing. Jesus obtained all of these at the Cross; this being true, then the question asked earlier as to whether it is God's will to heal is incorrect. After learning what you have just read, the question should be restructured to ask, "How do I access what Jesus provided for at the Cross in order to be healed?" The answer is to simply remember that Jesus paid the price for your healing at the Cross. Everything is paid for, completely finished, and consumed.

Who is the Agent Who Ministers Healing to Our Bodies?

The Holy Spirit is the agent that ministers healing. If we go back to the beginning of creation, He was the One who breathed life into man; the One who shaped a body out of dust and breathed into his nostrils the life of God—the One who breathed life into his muscles, nervous system, circulatory system, etc. It all gained life when His divine breath touched it. Consequently, it is logical to receive healing through the Holy Spirit, who sustains the human body in holiness and health and also ministers strength when it is weak.

> *But if the Spirit of Him who raised Jesus from the dead dwells in you, He who raised Christ from the dead will also give life to your mortal bodies through His Spirit who dwells in you.*
> **ROMANS 8:11**

The Holy Spirit lives in us. He is the same power that raised Jesus from the dead. The Messiah was beaten. His body became a boil for us. He gave up every drop of His blood. And after three days and two nights in the tomb, the Spirit of life of God raised Him once more. Now, that same Spirit dwells in us, continually vivifying our body.

> Divine healing doesn't teach we have an immortal body; it teaches we have an immortal life within a mortal body.

While the Holy Spirit, who raised Jesus' body from the tomb, dwells in our body, we will always have the power we need to raise ourselves up from every sickness; to stay healthy, strong, and functioning effectively until the day God calls us into His presence. If this Spirit raised the body of Jesus, then no infirmity or condition exists that He can't heal. The same will happen to us as it did with Jesus. He will anoint and heal us.

> ...Always carrying about in the body the dying of the Lord Jesus, that the life of Jesus also may be manifested in our body. For we who live are always delivered to death for Jesus' sake, that the life of Jesus also may be manifested in our mortal flesh. **2 CORINTHIANS 4:10, 11**

Divine health and physical healing allow the resurrection of Jesus to manifest in our mortal bodies. Not only does it live in us, but it also manifests in a visible and tangible way. We have the resurrected life in our mortal bodies! Although our bodies are not immortal, we have enough of it to be healed and to keep us healthy. This is a higher level than healing. Let us live on Earth serving God with a completely healed and healthy body!

Testimony: Maria Elena, 53 years old, suffered an accident at work ten years ago. Her left ankle broke in three parts and the tibia in two. She had to be operated and had screws placed in her ankle and an iron rod for the bone. Later on, she could still walk but was unable to jump or run. During a regular worship service at our church, her arms and legs began to tremble under the power of the Holy Spirit. She felt the bones in her left leg begin to shift, to straighten on their own. Suddenly, her legs began to run in place. She left her seat and proved she had been healed. She ran and jumped. That day, Maria Elena received a miracle in her life through the work of the Holy Spirit.

What Means Does the Holy Spirit Use to Heal Us?

The most common method used by the Holy Spirit to heal us is the Word of God.

He sent His word and healed them, and delivered them from their destructions. **PSALMS 107:20**

The Holy Spirit sent His Word in answer to that cry. As we read these verses, we find three important points that merit mention: He saved them, delivered them, and healed them. Salvation, deliverance, and healing came through His Word.

> When the Holy Spirit and the Word join forces, God's creative power is made available to everyone.

...Give attention to my words; incline your ear to my sayings. Do not let them depart from your eyes; keep them in the midst of your heart; For they are life to those who find them, and health to all their flesh. **PROVERBS 4:20-22**

These verses clarify that you cannot be sick and healthy at the same time. Both cannot operate in the same body simultaneously. Therefore, I suggest you choose health because that is God's will for you.

Testimony: A pregnant woman's unborn baby was diagnosed with Down syndrome. She fasted and prayed day and night; declaring God's healing word over her unborn child. One day, she saw our television program in which I declared the healing word over the audience. When she heard me say that I was about to pray for healing over everyone watching, she placed her hands on the TV screen, confessed, and believed the Word I spoke. The following week, when the baby was retested, the diagnosis was that the baby was in excellent health. The baby was normal.

How to Receive Your Healing and Live in Health

God's Word is medicine to your body; hence the importance to meditate on what it says, believe it, and confess it daily. This is the divine prerequisite to receiving your healing and living in health.

> *Beloved, I pray that you may prosper in all things and be in health, just as your soul prospers.* **3 JOHN 1:2**

John writes to a man called Gaius, a faithful man who lived in integrity. Inspired by the Holy Spirit, John declared that God's will is not to impose a sickness on our bodies only to heal us later; it is for us to live in continuously good health. I have discovered it is much easier to live healthily than to get healed; hence, living healthily is a decision we must make. Some people believe the best God has to offer is healing, but the best in God, beyond His ability to heal us, is His ability to keep us in a permanent state of wellbeing. He can make it possible for us never to get sick.

> *But the word is very near you, in your mouth and in your heart, that you may do it.* **DEUTERONOMY 30:14**

The secret is in keeping His Word in your heart; to practice it, confess it, and obey it. That is what God said to Joshua:

> *This Book of the Law shall not depart from your mouth, but you shall meditate in it day and night, that you may observe to do according to all that is written in it. For then you will make your way prosperous, and then you will have good success.* **JOSHUA 1:8**

From Deuteronomy and Joshua we conclude that prosperity, health, and success are closely related to our attitude towards

29

His Word. If we confess the Word and obey it, we will live in health and prosperity. This is indicative that our decision to have a good attitude concerning His Word must be made daily. Moses speaks on the same subject:

> *See, I have set before you today life and good, death and evil...* **DEUTERONOMY 30:15**

Confess God's Word; it is where we find the power of life and death to live in health. This is a personal decision!

> *Death and life are in the power of the tongue, and those who love it will eat its fruit.* **PROVERBS 18:21**

Many people are sick because they continually confess their sickness. Remember, they are what they speak.

> *I call heaven and earth as witnesses today against you, that I have set before you life and death, blessing and cursing; therefore choose life, that both you and your descendants may live...* **DEUTERONOMY 30:19**

The power to choose the path to sickness or health, to life or death, is in our mouths. The choice is ours. By our negative confessions, we choose sickness, destruction, and more; but by our faith-filled confessions, in line with God's Word, we choose life. When we understand His Word and meditate on it, it penetrates our hearts. After that, the only thing left for us to do is obey it. This is how we choose blessings instead of curses; health instead of death. God's Word teaches in the New Testament that Jesus is life. This being so, how can we allow sickness to destroy that life in us? God gave us the ability to choose between life and death, blessings and curses. He said, "You choose." Most believers have no idea that it is within their power to choose. But this does not surprise me as much as noticing that many, knowing, fail to choose life and blessings. I cannot conceive that people who know God have no idea how to make the right choice! They are always confessing death and curses.

> A grave curse upon God's people is lethargy; to be passive and do nothing.

God said that being lethargic and doing nothing is to die. The hungry lepers who thought it was worth the risk to enter the enemy camp before dying of hunger, made the decision and a corresponding action:

And when these lepers came to the outskirts of the camp, they went into one tent and ate and drank... **2 KINGS 7:8**

Right now, I want to speak to you! I want you to choose life and blessings. To do that, begin to say, "In Jesus' name, I am healed. He paid for my sickness. By His stripes, I am healed." Begin to confess these words and watch how God's Word becomes medicine to your bones and body. You will be healed by the confession of your mouth.

Testimony: A few years ago, a young man was involved in an automobile accident and was in a coma for several days. The doctors diagnosed him and declared him brain-dead. A couple from our church prayed for him in his hospital bed, declaring the healing word over his body. They visited him daily. Every day, they declared the word. After a few days of doing the same, the young man woke up from the coma, completely healed. Declaring the Word activated the power of God to revive him.

We must stand up and choose blessings, even against those who choose curses. Do not allow the enemy to step on you. Repeat after me: "I want life, health, prosperity, and success."

> ...The righteousness of faith speaks in this way, 'Do not say in your heart, 'Who will ascend into heaven?'' (that is, to bring Christ down from above) or, 'Who will descend into the abyss?' (that is, to bring Christ up from the dead). But what does it say? 'The word is near you, in your mouth and in your heart' (that is, the word of faith which we preach): that if you confess with your mouth the Lord Jesus and believe in your heart that God has raised Him from the dead, you will be saved. For with the heart one believes unto righteousness, and with the mouth confession is made unto salvation.
> **ROMANS 10:6-10**

Paul declares Moses' words where he relates the mouth with the heart, three times. The first two times, he speaks of the mouth in the first place, but the third time, he places the heart in the first place. The word salvation includes the soul, deliverance, protection, healing, strength, prosperity, joy, peace, and more; and it also includes the blessings Jesus obtained through His death at the Cross.

How Do We Receive the Benefits of Salvation?

Salvation is confessed with the mouth. Each benefit that is made available to us through Jesus' death is received through vocal confession and heartfelt faith. This is one way to take hold of the benefit Jesus provided for us at the Cross. We don't have to feel it; we just have to confess it with faith.

Do you believe the veracity of God's Word? Then you are ready to believe that by His stripes you are healed. You may not feel it; perhaps your body declares something different because pain testifies to your sickness. However, remember that you are not waiting on a feeling. The Holy Spirit, through your faith-filled confession, testifies of your healing. Declare your healing by faith. Stand up, declare it, and receive what is rightfully yours by inheritance. Again, I say to you, your blessings begin in your mouth, not your heart. When you confess it, on the third time it will go to the heart.

Review

If you are among those who questioned if God heals today, if His power is available for everyone, or if He can heal any physical, emotional, or mental illness—in other words, if it is God's will to heal every one of every sickness—you should have no more doubts or questions regarding this subject now.

- Healing is part of God's nature, and it is revealed through Jesus and His redeeming work at the Cross.

- Sickness is a demonic perversion of the perfect and creative work of God. It is a curse.

- The origin of every illness is demonic; hence, Jesus rebuked demons when healing the people.

- The agent that ministers divine healing to man is the Holy Spirit.

- The Holy Spirit heals though God's Word.

- The secret to living healthily is keeping His Word in our hearts, confessing it audibly, and practicing it daily.

■ To be healed, we must choose life, not death; health not
    sickness.

We have three witnesses that testify of God's Word with
respect to His will to heal: God's nature says, "I am your
physician, your doctor, the Lord that heals you. I do not
change." The Father anointed the Son with the Holy Spirit
and healed all who were oppressed by the devil. In essence,
Jesus said, "I came to do my Father's will. If you see me,
then you have seen my Father." At the Cross, He sealed His
will by taking our sin, transgressions, illness, and pain upon
Himself. He took our place. He was the supreme substitute
who carried our rebellion, pain, and sin because that is what
we needed to happen in order to receive His benefits and
blessings as His children.

God has given you a choice: life or death, blessings or curses.
He also asks that you believe His Word. What is your next
step? Simply to repeat the following, *"Lord, I choose health.
I choose life. I choose blessings, prosperity, peace, and joy.
These are my choices."*

Dear friend, right there where you are, I ask you to repeat
the following, *"Lord Jesus, right now I ask you to forgive
me for the negative words I have spoken throughout my life
against my body and loved ones. I repent of every idle word
I have spoken and every curse I have declared. I ask you to
forgive me; in the name of Jesus, amen!"*

Now, I ask you to believe and receive the healing that
belongs to you. Allow me to pray for you: *"Heavenly Father,
in the name of Jesus, I pray for the person reading this book
to receive healing. You earned that healing at the Cross. I*

declare you healed, right now. By His stripes you are healed. Amen!"

Note:
To pray with Apostle Guillermo Maldonado and receive his powerful impartation, visit: kingjesus.org/jesus-heals-prayer

CHAPTER II

IS IT GOD'S WILL TO HEAL YOU?

*W*hen God's Word affirms the declaration, "By His stripes we are healed," He includes everyone without exception. The Word does not exclude anyone. On the contrary, the prophet Isaiah declared, *"All we like sheep have gone astray; we have turned, everyone, to his own way; and the LORD has laid on Him (Jesus) the iniquity (sicknesses) of us all."*

Many people believe God heals, but they also claim He only heals some and not all who are sick. This belief has spread throughout the Church because, when the sick are prayed for by others, not all receive healing. Instead of continuing to pray and believe in God for a miracle, they come up with explanations for why they did not receive healing that later form part of their doctrine. This is understandable because the same happens in reference to salvation—when the altar call is made, not everyone comes forth. Salvation has nothing to do with whether or not God wants to save everyone; rather, salvation is a personal choice. The same goes for healing. The Word affirms this statement:

> *...Not willing that any should perish but that all should come to repentance.* **2 PETER 3:9**

Why Doesn't Everyone Receive Healing?

We know it is God's will to heal, but not everyone receives their healing because they fail to comply with the conditions required to activate His power. God's promises are conditional and dependent on the actions we must take to make them materialize. If the conditions are not met, God cannot deliver the blessings. However, this does not mean that it is not God's will to heal. The Lord knows that sick people cannot fight battles or carry out His will effectively. He knows that weak people cannot walk in His perfect plan and purpose. Sick people can neither praise and worship nor preach His Word freely. For these reasons, He reveals His will by telling us He can and wants to heal everyone of every disease. However, erroneous teachings concerning healing are very damaging, as they keep His children in darkness and ignorance, blinding them to what they have a right to claim and how to do so. It is impossible to claim one of God's promises if we are not sure that He is freely offering them; thus, the people perish for lack of knowing God's will.

> It is impossible to claim God's promise
> when His will is unknown.

If we lead a sinner to confess the sinner's prayer before he has the conviction that God wants to save him, it will be impossible to for him to be saved. An individual's faith begins when he discovers God's will.

Testimony: A woman was abandoned by her husband, leaving her with three children to raise by herself. She was suffering with respiratory problems, fever, and chest pain. One day while she was home alone, she decided to lay down on the floor and rest her head on a pillow. She turned on the television, and fell asleep. Around 10 o'clock that night, she heard my voice (and my translator) say, "Blanca, Blanca! Wake up! Don't go to sleep!" Half awake, she sat up and finished listening to the preaching and repeated a prayer she cannot remember today. Immediately, the Holy Spirit healed her. The next day she woke up completely healed of the fever and with no pain in her chest. Praise God!

Is God Real and Is He a Keeper of His Word?

God is not a man that He should lie nor a son of man that He should repent. Has He said, and will He not do? Or has He spoken, and will He not make it good? **NUMBERS 23:19**

Men often make promises they do not intend or are unable to keep only to repent later because the promises prove to be more difficult to fulfill than they had expected. God, however, is not like men. He has the power to carry out His promises, and when He promises something, He does it! Knowing this, why do we question if God can or wants to keep His promises? Has He ever lied? Has He ever taken back or broken a promise?

Illustration: When we seek employment, we visit several places, present countless resumes, and are interviewed by numerous people; and when we are finally hired, the supervisor informs us of our duties, our salary, and the payment schedule. We then go home, happily sharing the good news with our families, even making plans with the money we expect to earn before we start the job or receive the first paycheck! In this case, we trust the word of a man that never showed us his financial statements, check book, or bank account. And yet we believe he has the money, that he will keep his word, and that he will pay us what he promised. Now I ask you, "If we trust the word of a man, how can we not trust the Word of God?" If He said that by His stripes we are healed, we should and must believe that His Word is truth and that He will keep His promise.

The devil has been lying to us, saying that God's Word is a lie, that God makes us sick to prove our faith, and that His promises are not for us but for the holy ones. We must rebuke and reject that lie! From the onset, God promised to be our Healer and Physician, and He has not changed. His will has always been, is, and will continue to be: to heal His people.

41

How Can We Be Certain That God's Promise Will Be Carried Out in Us?

Thus God, determining to show more abundantly to the heirs of promise the immutability of His counsel, confirmed it by an oath, that by two immutable things, in which it is impossible for God to lie, we might have strong consolation, who have fled for refuge to lay hold of the hope set before us. **HEBREWS 6:17, 18**

The two immutable and unchanging things are:

- God's Word
- God's promises

God spoke and confirmed His word with a promise; this should comfort us because it is one way to ensure He will keep His promise to heal us of every illness and disease. In the Old and New Testaments, we learn that God healed every type of disease and everyone who was sick.

■ **God promised to heal all our diseases.**

Who forgives all your iniquities, who heals all your diseases... **PSALMS 103:3**

■ **God healed every Jew leaving Egypt.**

Interestingly, over three million Jews left Egypt and Crossed the desert, and there was not one sick person among them. The people wandered for forty years in the desert, and God provided one miracle after another in their favor. If God did it then, He will do it now. Many are sick today, tormented with diverse illnesses because of the lies presented by misinformed preachers who convince their congregations that divine healing is not for today; they assure God no longer heals and that if He does, He will heal some but not all. The Old Testament teaches that three million were healed. How many more can we expect to be healed after experiencing the redeeming work of Jesus?

Testimony: Juanita was born with a heart murmur—an intraventricular condition. Her mother was told that the baby would have to undergo major surgery if the problem was not resolved in six months. Invited by her aunt, Juanita's mother visited the church and received the Lord. She later brought her daughter Juanita; she was only a week old at the time. I prayed for her, and two weeks later, she flew to Colombia where a doctor confirmed that Juanita's heart condition had healed and surgery would no longer be necessary. The mother left Egypt—symbolic of the world—and God healed her baby daughter just as He healed the Israelites.

■ **Jesus established His will is to heal.**

Now a leper came to Him, imploring Him, kneeling down to Him and saying to Him, 'If You are willing, You can make me clean.' Then Jesus, moved with compassion, stretched out His hand and touched him, and said to him, 'I am willing; be cleansed.' **MARK 1:40, 41**

Jesus affirms two very important things:

• Yes, it is God's will to heal

• Yes, He has the power to do so

■ Jesus healed everyone

...They brought to Him many who were demon-possessed. And He cast out the spirits with a word, and healed all who were sick... **MATTHEW 8:16**

One obstacle preventing people from receiving their healing is doubt. They wonder if God wants to heal everyone. As previously stated, it is impossible to claim a blessing if we are unsure of His intention to give it to us; hence, we must stop our ignorance concerning God's promises and learn what they are and how to receive them. We cannot be ignorant of His Word, for He is the living God in whom we believe and trust.

...The whole multitude sought to touch Him, for power went out from Him and healed them all. **LUKE 6:19**

If Jesus healed every one that was sick, what makes us think He has changed?

Jesus Christ is the same yesterday, today, and forever. **HEBREWS 13:8**

■ The apostles also healed the sick

And the multitudes with one accord heeded the things spoken by Philip, hearing and seeing the miracles which he did. For unclean spirits, crying with a loud voice, came out of many who were possessed; and many who were paralyzed, and lame were healed. And there was great joy in that city. **ACTS 8:6–8**

When we preach about Jesus and His sacrifice at the Cross, in which He willingly surrendered His life for us, the blessings of salvation, healing, and deliverance comes to those who believe. When God's Word is preached and people receive it, they learn of their benefits, faith is imparted, and they are healed. This method is flawless; it never fails.

> Faith cannot be exercised if we ignore
> His good and perfect will for us.

■ James defines God's will

Is anyone among you sick? Let him call for the elders of the church, and let them pray over him, anointing him with oil in the name of the Lord. JAMES 5:14

James asked the question as if it was common for people to be sick, and he teaches whom we should call when it happens. In my experience, I have found that the context of this verse has been completely disobeyed by the Church. Generally, the elders are never called to pray for the sick, lay hands, anoint with oil, or declare anyone healed. For the most part, elders serve in the administrative rather than the spiritual area of the church. However, according to the Word, this is not the function that was carried out by the elders of the primitive church.

■ Jesus healed every illness

And Jesus went about all Galilee, teaching in their synagogues, preaching the gospel of the kingdom, and healing all kinds of sickness and all kinds of disease among the people. MATTHEW 4:23

Another translation states that Jesus healed all illnesses and infirmities. As we read the Gospels, we learn that the people brought those who were sick with all types of sickness, and Jesus never rejected anyone. He always prayed over them, declared their healing, and gave hope to those who approached Him.

Testimony: While preaching in Havana, Cuba, God led me to pray for the sick. His power descended upon that place, and I called forth those who had received healing. Among the people was a woman who had fallen from a building, breaking her leg in such a way that cutting an inch off the bone was the only means to save it. This caused her to limp and suffer every day. When God's power came upon her, she began to walk normally, without limping. She knew God had given her a creative miracle by lengthening her leg by an inch. Furthermore, her miracle caused the faith of those around her to increase and receive their miracles as well. Everyone was healed! That was one of several times I have seen God heal all who were sick. People received their miracles and were healed of cists, tumors, back pain, cancer, flat feet, blindness, deafness, and much more.

With all the verses, we have read on healing, I am certain many of you continue to say, "Yes Pastor, but my sickness is life-threatening and long-lived. It is difficult for God to heal me." Allow me to tell you that this type of mentality attributes more power to the sickness than to the Creator of our bodies. Renounce and reject all doubt, and embrace God's faith to believe that He wants to heal you and that your miracle is possible today!

Testimony: During a healing crusade held at my church, a lady with a condition called Chronic Hidradenitis came forward—an ailment that affects the skin, producing inflammation and a discharge of pus in the underarm region. Her condition was so severe that she was unable to carry her young son or sleep due to the pain and discomfort. I prayed for her and the Lord healed her completely. Instantly, the condition disappeared, and her skin returned to normal.

How Does Faith Enter the Heart?

So then faith comes by hearing, and hearing by the word of God. **ROMANS 10:17**

Faith comes from hearing God's Word continuously, and note that the key word here is *continuously* because it produces faith to believe. Faith does not enter the heart through sympathy, by talking about an illness, or through psychology; it comes by constantly hearing God's Word on healing. If we want people to have faith in a certain area, we must teach them what the Word says concerning said area. Likewise, if we want them to learn about prosperity, then we must teach them about prosperity. If we want them to learn to pray, we must teach them about prayer. If we want them to develop faith in the area of healing, we must teach them all there is to know about healing according to His Word. Otherwise, no one will have the faith to receive their individual miracle.

If faith comes by hearing, we can then conclude that doubt comes by hearing as well. Today, many people speak in doubt. They complain of being sick and tired and whine about their conditions; thus, solidifying the condition with the confession. Their failure to declare God's Word fills their hearts with doubt, making it difficult for them to receive physical healing.

What is the Solution for People to Receive Their Healing?

If we want people to receive their healing, we must teach them the truth about healing; it is the only way to believe and to be healed.

> *And you shall know the truth, and the truth shall make you free.* JOHN 8:32

What is the Truth about Healing?

God is our Healer; it is in His nature to heal. Jesus came and died at the Cross for the wages of our sins and sicknesses. When He was raised from the dead, He commanded us to continue His ministry of healing the sick.

> *...They will lay hands on the sick, and they will recover.* MARK 16:18

We do not doubt God's ability to save even the worst of sinners. How can we be so sure?

> *For God so loved the world that He gave His only begotten Son, that whoever believes in Him should not perish but have everlasting life.* JOHN 3:16

If we teach the truth about healing, people will believe in it the same way they believe in salvation. When we do this, no one will lack the knowledge to receive healing. God wants spiritual and physical healing for every one of His children; this, because He needs our bodies to carry out His perfect will on Earth as we preach the Gospel of Jesus Christ.

> *...You were bought at a price; therefore glorify God in your body and in your spirit...* 1 CORINTHIANS 6:20

Sickness destroys the body, whose price was paid for by the precious blood of Jesus. Therefore, we must rebel against infirmities and declare healing for our bodies in the name of Jesus.

Testimony: During another healing crusade held in our ministry, a woman bound to a wheelchair was brought to me. Her doctors had diagnosed her with bone cancer. She had spent the preceding nine months unable to walk and three of those months with a tumor in her liver. Her body was being eaten by sickness. When I prayed for her, she felt the power of God touch her, and she stood up from the wheelchair without help. Now she is completely healed by the Lord's supernatural power, and she can do everything the sickness had prevented her from doing!

Salvation from sin and physical healing are blessings provided by the sacrifice of Jesus at the Cross. We can claim our salvation and healing because His sacrifice covers both blessings. The blessing would be incomplete if we could be saved but could not receive the healing.

> You cannot accept only part of the benefits after hearing this truth.

...It is the power of God to salvation for everyone who believes... **ROMANS 1:16**

The Greek word for salvation is *soteria*; it means deliverance, protection, strength, healing, provision, and so much more. Jesus often used this word to refer to salvation, deliverance, and healing.

...He said to her, 'Daughter, your faith has made you well. Go in peace, and be healed of your affliction.' **MARK 5:34**

Once again, healing is part of the whole package given by the redeeming work of Jesus at the Cross. He carried our sicknesses, He took our place and delivered our bodies from every illness and ailment, and He also paid for our sins and saved us from spending eternity in hell.

Surely He has borne our griefs and carried our sorrows...
ISAIAH 53:4

If Jesus did it all, we should no longer carry the burden of any illness, and every believer should enjoy total health.

Testimony: A man had spent eight months—24 hours a day—connected to an oxygen tank. He was dependent upon oxygen due to Pulmonary Fibrosis, a condition that causes the scarring or enlargement of the lungs. The lungs become rigid, making it difficult to breathe. The first time he visited our church, he received Jesus as Lord and Savior of his life. When he answered the altar call, he took a bold step of faith and removed his oxygen mask, and God healed him. For the first time in eight months, he was able to breathe normally. The salvation of his soul produced healing to his body. And so, there is healing in the forgiveness of our sins!

Review

It is God's desire to save everyone, not just a few. We must claim our healing because God promised to heal all who were sick. He is real, and He promised to heal our sicknesses, infirmities, and diseases, as He did for the Israelites—by His word and in His name. When Jesus died at the Cross, He took upon Himself our sins and infirmities; with His resurrection, He obtained the power to defeat and destroy them; and then He commissioned the apostles to continue His ministry. However, for people to learn and receive this truth, we must preach and teach it because faith comes by hearing and hearing by the Word of God. Only then will we be free.

Many people fail to receive healing because they believe God has the power to heal anyone who is sick, except for them. In this chapter, we learned that:

- God's will is to heal everyone.

- God created us to establish His Kingdom on Earth, and He knows we cannot do this if we are sick. He wants His children healthy.

- God keeps His promises. He promised to heal us, and He is not a man to lie or the son of man to change His mind.

- Satan is a liar, telling people the false doctrine that God sends sickness to prove our faith, love, and faithfulness.

- God's Word and promises are unchanging. If He promised to heal us, He will certainly keep His word.

- Jesus healed every sick person that approached Him.

- Jesus empowered the apostles to heal in His name.

- Our faith increases when we continuously hear God's Word.

- To accept salvation but not healing is to accept only part of the benefits provided by His sacrifice at the Cross.

Note:
To pray with Apostle Guillermo Maldonado and receive his powerful impartation, visit: kingjesus.org/jesus-heals-prayer

CHAPTER III

THE CAUSE OF SICKNESS AND ITS RELATIONSHIP WITH DEMONS

ealing is a promise of God. I do not know if it is you, a loved one, or a close friend that might be suffering with a physical ailment, but I do know God's plan for you: to live a full and abundant life. I am also certain that all things are possible to those who believe. I am unaware of your doctor's diagnosis, but I have the conviction that the One whose name is above every name exists: Jesus! The mention of His name alone makes every spirit of sickness run.

Scientists struggle to discover solutions for rare and countless physical conditions, depending solely on science and technology. Although these are valid and useful resources that have proven valuable in determining the cause of many illnesses, in many cases they also prove to be insufficient. They may be helpful in discovering palliative methods, but that is not always the case because the root of these incurable diseases is spiritual. I am referring to those diseases caused by spiritual influences or demonic activity. The Church has a similar problem. We often try to deal with a sickness in the body by dealing with the physical problem rather than the spiritual. Therefore, we fail to deal with the true root of the problem. This is the reason many are sick, in despair, or have died prematurely.

This chapter covers the relationship between sickness and demons; knowing this will lead to the root of the problem which in turn leads to healing. In simple terms, we must stop dealing with the cobwebs and start dealing with the spider. The spider is the root of the problem, the web is the result; let us deal with the root and not the outcome.

What is the Root of Sickness?

To explain the root of sickness I will begin by saying that every disease has a life of its own. It has a biological germ or agent that makes it work; an evil life form, which did not come from God, capable of destroying the human body. Since it does not come from God, it is safe to say that it comes from Satan. The evil life or spirit of infirmity breathes life into the sickness, making it develop and destroy everything in its path—the Holy Spirit operates the same way, only instead of taking life it breathes the breath of life upon each body.

Our spirit and body are separated when our physical body dies, leaving the body to return to dust. The same takes place when a spirit of infirmity or sickness is rebuked; the sickness dies and returns to wherever it came from.

With this we can conclude that many sicknesses begin with a small germ, a satanic life form sent to possess and destroy the body. As long as this spirit is allowed to dwell in the body, the development of the viral agent continues uninterrupted in its destructive path. However, as soon as the spirit of infirmity is casted out, in the name of Jesus, the development and progress of this agent is stopped, and it dies; only then can the healing process begin. When the lifeline of the infirmity is rebuked, its effects soon come to an end.

Cancer is a living, satanic entity; many doctors agree with this. If anyone rebukes the life or the root of cancer, the physical effects caused by the cancer will disappear. When a sickness enters the body, an internal battle begins between the life of God and the satanic life. The solution to this is to have faith in the supernatural power of God and to cast out the sickness. When I pray for people suffering with cancer, I curse the cancerous life and its root. I also order the physical restoration of every part of the body that was damaged by it. Time after time, I have seen people completely recover.

Three Spirits that Produce Cancer

- The spirit of death
- The spirit of infirmity
- The spirit of cancer

What is the answer? Rebuke them and the physical body will be healed. Up to now, we can conclude two things: sickness comes from Satan and not from God, and believers have the power and authority to rebuke the spirits that cause the illness. Let us take charge and rebuke the spirit of infirmity out of those who are sick, and watch them recover and be healed.

"Every year, the American Cancer Society estimates the number of new cases of cancer and the deaths that will occur in the United States in the current year; it compiles the most recent information of incidences, mortality, and survival based on the data reported by the National Cancer Institute, Centers for Control and Prevention, the North American Association of Central Registry for Cancer, and the mortality rates reported by the National Center for Health Statistics. It is projected that in 2009, in the United States, 1,479,350 new cases of cancer and 562,340 deaths by cancer will be reported. Even though we have made progress in reducing the incidence rate of mortality and improved the chances of survival, cancer continues to be the biggest contributor to death, more so than heart disease in people under 85. More progress can be made by applying the knowledge acquired to control cancer throughout every sector in society and supporting research in the prevention, early detection, and treatment of cancer." [1]

Per this article, doctors struggle to educate themselves, and prevent and treat the effects of cancer, but they have yet to discover the cause of it. The reason for this is because they are dealing with cancer solely on the physical level, disregarding the fact that the root of this sickness is a spiritual one.

Important Information on HIV

- The global percentage of adults who live with HIV has stabilized since 2000.

- In 2007, 2.7 million new cases of people infected with HIV and 2 million deaths related to this virus were reported.

- The rate of spread for this disease has declined in various countries, but at the global level these favorable tendencies are, at least, partially compensated by the increase of spread in other countries.

- Surveys show that in 14 out of 17 African countries, the percentage of young pregnant women (15 - 24), who are infected with HIV, declined in 2000-2001. According to the Declaration of Commitment, the reduction of spread of infectious diseases in 7 countries has equaled or exceeded the objective of 25% for 2010.

- Due to a higher rate of access and treatment during the last 10 years, the number of deaths caused by AIDS has declined.

- Sub-Saharan Africa continues to be the region most affected by HIV, with 67% of its population living with HIV and 75% of deaths by AIDS in 2007. However, the most

1   CA Cancer J Clin 2009. © 2009 American Cancer Society, Inc. http://caonline. amcancersoc.org/

worrisome increase of new infections is taking place in populated countries in other regions including: Indonesia, the Russian Federation, and various other countries with a high-income ratio.

■ At the global level, the percentage of women infected with HIV has remained stable (at 50%) the last few years. However, the percentage of women contaminated is increasing in various countries.

■ In almost every region of Sub-Saharan Africa, HIV infects drug addicts who use syringes, homosexual men, and those working in any sex-related business. [2]

Even if these statistics show some advances in the prevention and control of this disease, they fail to announce a cure. Modern science has been unsuccessful in finding a cure for this contagious disease that is killing so many people—only the power of Jesus can eradicate this virus from the body of men, women, and children.

What Was Jesus' Ministry?

From beginning to end, Jesus operated in four areas or dimensions:

■ Preaching
■ Teaching
■ Healing the sick
■ Rebuking demons

> And Jesus went about all Galilee, teaching in their synagogues, preaching the gospel of the kingdom, and healing all kinds of sickness and all kinds of disease among the people. Then His fame went throughout all Syria; and

2 2008 Report on the global AIDS epidemic: Chapter 2 http://www.unaids.org

they brought to Him all sick people who were afflicted with various diseases and torments, and those who were demon-possessed, epileptics, and paralytics; and He healed them.
MATTHEW 4:23, 24

These four areas are the physical manifestation of the visible Kingdom of God on Earth. Today, we only practice the first two: We preach and teach but fail to heal the sick or cast out demons. When we read about Jesus demonstrating the Kingdom of God, we notice that He always operated in the four dimensions, which imply that the Kingdom's power was manifested.

■ Jesus continued in His ministry

When the sun was setting, all those who had any that were sick with various diseases brought them to Him; and He laid His hands on every one of them and healed them. ...demons also came out of many, crying out and saying, 'You are the Christ, the Son of God!' And He, rebuking them, did not allow them to speak, for they knew that He was the Christ.
LUKE 4:40, 41

Once more, we see the deliverance ministry and the healing ministry working together as one. People went to Jesus because they were sick, but in many cases, the healing required the expulsion of demons. The same is noted when Jesus laid hands on the sick—this is a Biblical method to heal the sick and cast out demons.

■ Jesus healed the woman that was bent over

Now He was teaching in one of the synagogues on the Sabbath. And behold, there was a woman who had a spirit of infirmity eighteen years, and was bent over and could in no way raise herself up. **LUKE 13:10, 11**

This verse mentions another incident in the ministry of Jesus that took place in the synagogue. The woman's sickness was caused by demons, causing her body to bend over; thus, preventing her from raising herself up. It is important to note a few relevant aspects of this incident:

- The root of her sickness was demonic.

...There was a woman who had a spirit of infirmity eighteen years, and was bent over and could in no way raise herself up. [...] So ought not this woman, being a daughter of Abraham, whom Satan has bound—think of it—for eighteen years, be loosed from this bond on the Sabbath? **LUKE 13:11, 16**

- Jesus discerned the cause of the sickness was spiritual, not physical.

We often find ourselves trying to treat an illness that originates in the spirit as if it were a common physical ailment. To avoid this, we need to ask the Lord for spiritual discernment. This is necessary if we want to see beyond the obvious corporal problem.

In the last decades, discernment has been substituted by psychology and faith by reason; this trend has led to the use of human methods to find answers for spiritual problems. Psychology, philosophy, and religion have been useful in dealing with the web of the problem but have failed to exterminate the spider. In other words, they deal with the manifestation of the symptoms rather than dealing with the root of the problem. For this reason, we need the discernment of the Holy Spirit and faith—no one can understand the human being unless it is through the revelation of the Creator.

- The woman had been bent over 18 years

Observe the satanic nature in this. We know the enemy came to kill, steal, destroy, and to cause people pain. In the passage we read, the spirit was causing the woman to live bent over, unable to raise her head.

Testimony: A young woman in Ecuador was suffering with scoliosis—an abnormal curvature of the spine. Her spinal cord was deformed causing her to lean to one side as she walked. When I prayed for her and rebuked the spirit of infirmity, she was healed, and her back was instantly straightened.

Some wicked spirits, similar to the one Jesus rebuked, cause bone pain, handicaps, paralysis, or intense pain. Every time I rebuke the spirit of pain, people are healed.

■ Jesus rebuked the spirit of deafness

When Jesus saw that the people came running together, He rebuked the unclean spirit, saying to it, 'Deaf and dumb spirit, I command you, come out of him and enter him no more!' Then the spirit cried out, convulsed him greatly, and came out of him. And he became as one dead, so that many said, 'He is dead.' **MARK 9:25, 26**

From personal experience, I can confirm that every time I pray for someone who is deaf, I rebuke the spirit causing it, as Jesus did.

Testimony: On a certain occasion, during a church service, I stepped off the pulpit and began walking down the aisles. As I did this, the Lord showed me there was a deaf person to my right. When I called that person to come forth, a young 21-year-old woman from Nicaragua stood up. She was born deaf. When I prayed for her, her ears were instantly opened, and her tongue was loosened. The miracle caused a great impact because she had never heard or spoken anything. She had to communicate through sign language. The miracle was so powerful that I asked her to give her testimony on television.

What terms should we use when praying against an illness?

Each medical condition or terminology has a corresponding spiritual name; in other words, doctors diagnose arthritis, and we rebuke the spirit of arthritis. Doctors diagnose blindness, and we rebuke the spirit of blindness. Doctors diagnose a dislocated spine or a hernia, and we rebuke the spirit of infirmity. What are we doing? While doctors deal with the physical aspects of the infirmity, we attack the spirit of infirmity and rebuke it from the human body. We have doctors in our congregation that do both and are getting amazing and glorious results.

If you discover a snake in your home, I am certain you will not treat it kindly. You will look for something you can use to kill it and get it out of the house. That is exactly what we have to do with demons causing pain and sickness in our bodies and in our loved one.

Testimony: During a miracle crusade, the Holy Spirit revealed to me by word of knowledge that two people had tried to commit suicide. When I called these people to come forth, two women went forward. The first young lady, a 21-year-old, said she wanted to end her life several times because she felt rejected by her parents and that there seemed to be no end to their discussions. In the worst of times, she tried to commit suicide by hiding in her bathroom and cutting her veins. On one of those attempts, she was pregnant with her second son. The second young lady, also 21, had tried to commit suicide three times; on one such occasion, she swallowed 74 pills. When she was found, she was taken to the hospital only to be released to try it again the following night. I prayed for them and rebuked the spirit of suicide; both were instantly delivered. Neither could have been helped by a psychologist or with antidepressants because the root of their problems was a spirit of suicide that wanted to end their lives. Where psychologists or doctors fail, God succeeds because nothing is impossible for Him.

God succeeds where men fail.

How Much Time did Jesus Invest Healing and Delivering the People?

On that very day, some Pharisees came, saying to Him, 'Get out and depart from here, for Herod wants to kill You.' And He said to them, 'Go, tell that fox, 'Behold, I cast out demons and perform cures today and tomorrow, and the third day I shall be perfected.' **LUKE 13:31, 32**

"...Today and tomorrow and the third day..." This beautiful Hebraic expression means: "From this day forward, I will work on it until I finish" (A Hebraism is a colloquial idiom used to properly express the Hebrew language). In essence, Jesus said He would do two things from that day forward: rebuke demons and heal the sick; it was then that His ministry took full force. From its onset to its completion, He did four things: preach, teach, heal, and rebuke demons. This is indicative that during his three and a half years in ministry, half of that time was spent on healing the sick and delivering the oppressed. Before His ascension, He delegated the same authority to his twelve and seventy disciples, and today He

is delegating it to us. He commands us to continue with His ministry. Countless are in bondage by demonic oppressions affecting their bodies, and we have the power and authority to heal and deliver them in His name; this is how we continue operating in the fullness of His ministry.

Testimony: On one occasion, an elder of our church shared with me that his mother-in-law had been diagnosed with breast cancer. We called her because she did not live in Miami. I prayed for her over the phone, rebuking the spirit of cancer and death. Today she testifies that she felt heat in her body the instant I prayed. The following week, I was told by the elder that his mother-in-law had visited the doctor. After the examination, the doctor could not understand how cancer could be there one day and gone the next. God healed her completely, and to this day she is still healed. Now we understand why Jesus used the same words, interchangeably, when dealing with a sickness or demonic oppression; both are closely related as shown by the testimony.

What is Included in the Salvation Jesus Gave Us?

Salvation has two important characteristics: It saves one's spirit and keeps us from eternal damnation; it also includes every aspect of human personality.

To understand this statement, let us study a few important principles and definitions:

Can We Be Sick in Our Whole Self?

Of course, we can! To have a better understanding of this, it is important to know that we are triune beings. We are a spirit with a soul (will, emotions, and mind), living in a physical body. With this in mind, the answer to the previous question makes more sense because now we know we can be sick in one or all of these areas (demons can affect any of them). There are five areas in us where we can get sick:

- **The body:** Physical ailments are easier to identify and diagnose; thus, providing a guide to finding a cure.

- **The mind:** The mind is a component of the soul; it is not the brain. People can suffer countless infirmities of the brain and still have clear, lucid minds and thought processes. Likewise, many people can feel physically healthy but suffer with mental illnesses. There are spirits of fear, anxiety, panic, hopelessness, depression, and more that can oppress the human mind.

- **The emotions:** These are normally referred to as feelings. When our emotions suffer, we can also experience the added agony of physical pain; this type of situation often allows spirits to oppress us, including: spirits of unforgiveness, bitterness, resentment, stubbornness, and hatred.

- **The will:** Many people are sick because they lack sufficient self control to make wise decisions. Jesus said the spirit is willing, but the flesh is not. Some symptoms that alert us of wicked spirits operating in people are: stubbornness, rebellion, a strong personality, and more.

- **The spirit:** In order to establish or restore a healthy relationship with God, our spirit must be healthy. Without a personal relationship with Jesus, our spirit may be sick or even dead due to sin. For this reason, we must repent of our sins and be born again.

A demonic presence can exist in every area of human personality, and we must learn to properly deal with it. This means we must apply the correct medication by means of the complete redeeming work at the Cross. Let us look at a few important definitions:

What is Sickness?

Sickness is an invasion and demonic perversion of the perfect and creative work of God. The devil uses sickness to torment every area of an individual's personality.

What is Healing?

The Bible uses three words to describe the concept of healing:

- **Iaomai:** to heal or make whole.

  Now it happened on a certain day, as He was teaching, that there were Pharisees and teachers of the law sitting by, who had come out of every town of Galilee, Judea, and Jerusalem. And the power of the Lord was present to heal them. LUKE 5:17

- **Therapeuo:** When this word is used in the Bible, it is connected to worship. From this we learn that one who worships can be healed instantly because worship unto the Lord is healing therapy.

- **Sozo:** to save a suffering one (from perishing), i.e. one suffering from disease, to make well, heal, restore to health. [3]

  This word is used when talking about deliverance from demons, the forgiveness of sins, healing of the body and soul, financial prosperity, protection, and more. The meaning of this word indicates that healing is for every area of human life. Furthermore, demons may have the

---

3 Blue Letter Bible. "Dictionary and Word Search for sozo (Strong's 4982". Blue Letter Bible. 1996-2009. 31 Jul 2009. <http://www.blueletterbible.og/lang/lexicon/lexicon.cfm?strongs=G4982>

ability to influence us in any area, but Jesus, through His death and redeeming work at the Cross, also provided healing in every area.

What is Included in the Redeeming Work of Jesus at the Cross?

...Jesus... said, 'It is finished!' And bowing His head, He gave up His spirit. **JOHN 19:30**

The phrase *"It is finished"* is the Greek word *teleo*, meaning to bring to a close, to finish, or to end; to execute, to complete, or to fulfill (so that the thing done corresponds to what has been said, the order, command etc.); to carry out the contents of a command. In other words, the debt was paid in full. The shout Jesus gave was one of victory, not pain, because He had carried out His command to completion. The debt of sin was completely canceled and paid for; then Jesus surrendered His Spirit and died.

At the Cross, Jesus paid the wages of our sins, rebellion, transgressions, iniquity, physical and mental infirmities, and all else that causes pain and suffering. There is nothing left to be paid. His work was perfect and complete, and it includes healing in body, soul, and spirit. If this is true, why do we continue to suffer with mental, physical, and emotional pain? Because we have yet to grab a hold of, by faith, the fullness of what Jesus did at the Cross.

How Can We Be Free from a Sickness Caused by a Demon?

If you then, being evil, know how to give good gifts to your children, how much more will your heavenly Father give the Holy Spirit to those who ask Him! And He was casting out a demon, and it was mute. So it was, when the demon had

gone out, that the mute spoke; and the multitudes marveled.
LUKE 11:13, 14

Note that Jesus introduced the Holy Spirit before rebuking the demons. He gave us His Spirit, first and foremost, to deal with demons, to bring conviction of sin, and to inform the world that Satan had been judged and defeated. The reason Jesus sent His Spirit was to give us the power to destroy every satanic work. The Holy Spirit gives us the discernment to discover the root and the power required to rebuke and cast out demons.

Who Gave Jesus the Power to Heal the Sick and Rebuke Demons?

But if I cast out demons by the Spirit of God, surely the kingdom of God has come upon you. **MATTHEW 12:28**

The Holy Spirit gave Jesus the divine power to heal the sick and cast out demons. The conclusion to this topic is that people can get sick in five areas: the body, the soul, the spirit, the emotions, and the will. For every area influenced by demonic spirits, the redeeming work of Jesus counterattacks and destroys all demonic undertaking, giving us total healing. The Holy Spirit gives us the ability to discern the origin of any sickness— physical, biological, or spiritual. Once we recognize the root of the problem, the Spirit empowers us to rebuke the demons, to produce creative miracles if the cause is biological, and to discover the cure if the root is of natural origin; in any case, if the cause is spiritual, directly or indirectly caused by demons, we can go to Jesus to grab a hold of and receive our healing.

Testimony: A lady was suffering with a bipolar disorder; a mental illness that is difficult to diagnose and very hard to control, with a high probability to become a chronic condition, and it is characterized by the evidence of depression, loss of interest, a feeling of worthlessness and hopelessness, guilt, and more. This condition also increases the risk of death by suicide. She suffered manic depression which is characterized by uncommon highs and lows in personality. One moment she felt sad and depressed; other times she was euphoric. During the low times, she would, at times, walk the streets naked. She had also tried to commit suicide. She was taking a high dose of prescription medication, but there is no cure for this condition. The lady presented the medical evidence certifying the professional diagnosis of the condition. Together with her husband, they accepted the Lord on their first visit to the church. They were baptized and then asked the Lord to heal her. In less than three months, the blessing of God's healing was evident. She was healed and no longer needed medication. Furthermore, she presented the church with documentation signed by a judge evidencing her healing and stating that she no longer needed a legal tutor or treatment. Her record was cleared! Once more it becomes evident that the origin of a mental condition was spiritual. The psychologists and psychiatrists were unable to help her because they were treating the mind and emotions rather than the spirit. The mental condition she suffered was the byproduct of the spiritual torture and oppression she was experiencing.

What is the Solution or Cure?

The rate of diseases affecting the world population increases exponentially each day. Modern science has made important discoveries in efforts to cure a few of them, but there are still millions who are sick and dying at an alarming rate.

The tragedy here is that the same illnesses are affecting Christians world-wide due to lack of knowledge in God's Word and of His perfect will. This is caused by the traditional teaching stating that sickness is a God-given punishment or that healing belongs to the era of the apostles, and it is not for today. Sicknesses are not of God; they are the devil's creation. God never changes—He healed yesterday, heals today, and will continue to heal for eternity. He does not use an illness to humble His people. In fact, Jesus came to heal, deliver, and save us, and He did it so we could live in total wellbeing: in body, soul, and spirit.

Testimony: Julissa suffered from depression from the age of seven until she was 15; she had tried to take her life because she felt unloved. Furthermore, she was suffering with rejection due to her parents' divorce. One night at church, she cried out to God: "If you don't show me that You are real, I will kill myself." At church, we prayed for her, rebuking the spirits of suicide, rejection, and depression. The following day, eight years of depression, rejection, and anger that would lead her to hurt herself and other children were finally a thing of the past. God healed her supernaturally. The depression left without medication. Consequently, rejection and the desire to commit suicide also left without the need for her to undergo psychological treatment. God did it all; again, we learn that the cause of depression was spiritual.

Review

This chapter covered the cause of sicknesses and their relationship with demonic activity. Scientists struggle to find a cure for many of them, and even though they are successful in making advancements, they are unable to keep up because new ones continue to appear.

- The origin of any illness is hell. Satan, not God, causes man to be sick.

- Sickness begins with a microscopic germ; it is the satanic life sent to possess the human body for the purpose of destroying it.

- Jesus' ministry had four components: preach, teach, heal the sick, and cast out demons.

- Jesus healed everyone, and He healed every disease He encountered.

- There is a spirit assigned to each sickness, for example: the spirit of cancer.

- The gift of salvation Jesus gave us includes healing for every area of our lives.

- There are five areas that can be potentially attacked by demonic sickness: the body, mind, emotions, will, and spirit.

- Sickness is a demonic invasion and perversion of God's perfect and creative work.

- At the Cross, Jesus paid for our sins and all types of sicknesses.

- To be free of any illness caused by demons, we must cast them out in the name of Jesus.

- The agent that empowered Jesus to cast out demons and heal the sick was the Holy Spirit, and He is with us today.

If you want to be free of any demonic oppression in your mind, body, or spirit repeat the following prayer aloud:

"Jesus, with all my heart, I repent for allowing Satan to come into my life and make me sick. I ask You to forgive me. Right

now, I take hold of the complete and perfect work fulfilled at the Cross. I declare myself healed, free, and saved. I renounce every spirit of infirmity and I order them to leave my body right now! I declare myself totally free in body, mind, spirit, emotions, and will. At this time, I choose to dedicate and consecrate my humanity to You; to serve You every day of my life. Amen!"

Note:

To pray with Apostle Guillermo Maldonado and receive his powerful impartation, visit: kingjesus.org/jesus-heals-prayer

CHAPTER IV

OBSTACLES THAT PREVENT YOUR HEALING

The Word is clear: There is no sickness in God; therefore, He cannot give us what He does not possess. The Word does say that God is health, abundant life, and our Healer. Also, the prophet Jeremiah affirms that God will bring health and healing. The prophet Isaiah is even more categorical when he says that by His stripes we are healed. Why, then, do some receive healing and others do not? Why are some instantly healed and others progressively healed?

I have had the opportunity to see thousands receive their healing by God's power and mercy—people of different races, gender, ages, and religious affiliations from many countries around the world. I have also seen hundreds of God's children, men and women of God, who live in holiness and are dedicated to the Lord, who did not receive their healing even after I prayed for them; this is hard for me to understand. Some even went home to be with the Lord after the sickness destroyed their bodies. There are things that I simply do not understand; hence, it is my responsibility as God's apostle to seek the divine revelation and teach it correctly to the people.

> The obstacles to receiving your healing
> are found on our side, not God's.

When Jesus died, the veil was ripped from top to bottom and every obstacle or barrier present on God's side was removed. There are countless obstacles in the life of a believer; some are placed by Satan and others by our decisions. For that reason, to be successful Christians, we must learn to destroy all of them.

Testimony: In our church, one of my ministers was diagnosed with cancer. We prayed for her and anointed her with oil. Sadly, although she enjoyed a temporary improvement in her health, the cancer returned. Once again, I fasted, prayed, and rebuked the spirit of cancer, but she still went home to be with the Lord. She died! This touched me deeply because I have seen countless people be healed of cancer during the crusades at church and in other nations, people who were terminally ill. In her case, it did not happen—she was very close to my heart. I finally felt in my heart that I needed to look for answers in the obstacles that keep people from receiving their healing.

What Common Obstacles Keep People from Receiving Their Healing?

After years in ministry, I discovered that removing the obstacles is equivalent to preparing the field in which people can meet the conditions required to receive their healing and live healthy for the rest of their lives.

These are the obstacles:

1. Ignorance

Lack of knowledge of God's Word and His perfect will is a big obstacle keeping us from receiving our healing. Countless Christians have no idea what the Word says about physical healing.

Therefore my people have gone into captivity, because they have no knowledge; Their honorable men are famished, And their multitude dried up with thirst. **ISAIAH 5:13**

Christians have yet to learn that God left His children an inheritance; most also lack the deep and complete truth concerning the work Jesus did on the Cross.

Lacking knowledge in any area of our lives is an open invitation to the enemy; he will take advantage of our condition and get the upper hand to destroy us.

The Word mentions two types of ignorance: the people who, for whatever reason, never had access to knowing the truth, and the people who, having countless opportunities to learn the truth and end their ignorance, chose to reject it. Both types of ignorance are detrimental, but the latter is worse than the former because it involves the individual's ability to choose and a bad decision. Ignorance is a sin because it is the end result of one's choice not to seek the truth, not to search the Word and discover what God has to say. We must confess this sin and ask God to forgive us.

Allow me to guide you in a prayer of repentance. Please repeat the following words aloud: *"Lord, I recognize that in many ways, I have ignored the truth of Your Word and Your perfect will due to negligence. Right now, I confess my sin and repent. Please forgive me. I commit myself to seek Your truth and obey it. From this day forward, I will do it diligently. Amen!"*

2. Doubt

Doubt is a very common obstacle in the church. It is usually viewed as a normal and harmless condition, but do you know what it is? God's Word calls it a sin. If we look at it for what it is, we become better prepared to rid ourselves of doubt and pave the way to believe in what God has for us. Understanding this is so important that I have dedicated an entire chapter on doubt. It will be viewed from two standpoints: as sin and as a demonic spirit.

3. Not confessing our sin

He who covers his sins will not prosper, but whoever confesses and forsakes them will have mercy. **PROVERBS 28:13**

Another obstacle that can keep us from our healing is not confessing our sin. We can struggle to succeed and set many goals for ourselves, but if we have hidden sin that needs forgiveness, we will never prosper. I am certain that many of us have sin in our lives for which we need to repent; sin we have tried to hide and forget about. Many people are under the impression that God will never find out what we did if we don't confess the sin; that is crazy because God knows everything! He wants our confession in order to forgive us, not because He needs to know what we did wrong. Our worse confession does not surprise God. Therefore, we cannot possibly shock Him because He knows everything, even our most intimate thoughts.

If we confess our sins, He is faithful and just to forgive us our sins and to cleanse us from all unrighteousness. **1 JOHN 1:9**

At this time, I would like to ask you to repeat this prayer of repentance for any sin you need to confess; please do it aloud: *"Lord Jesus, Your Word teaches that if we confess our sin and depart from it, You will show us Your mercy. Today, of my own free will and in the name of Jesus, I confess every sin of commission and omission. Forgive me, and now by faith, I receive your forgiveness. Amen!"* During your private time with God, confess aloud every sin you have tried to keep hidden in your heart, and receive your deliverance.

4. Unforgiveness

Unforgiveness is very common in the body of Christ—large percentages of people hold grudges and keep records of wrongdoings. Consequently, many are attacked by physical ailments or are physically weak; others have died.

And whenever you stand praying, if you have anything against anyone, forgive him, that your Father in heaven may also forgive you your trespasses. **MARK 11:25**

Living with resentment and unforgiveness raises a great barrier that blocks our prayers from reaching God's throne and keeps them from being answered. If we want to be clean vessels and have our prayers answered, we must first forgive and later pray. This is a personal decision we must make; therefore, we don't have to wait to feel something in order to carry it out. When we make the heartfelt decision to forgive, God gives us the grace to do it.

Testimony: One day, while ministering in a House of Peace, a lady asked me to pray for her. She was suffering with arthritis; her fingers were crooked, and she was unable to straighten them out. This condition caused her great pain. The instant I was about to pray, I felt in my heart that her condition was due to unforgiveness. Her choice not to forgive had given a wicked spirit the opportunity to oppress her. I called one of the ministers that had gone with me and asked her to help this lady to forgive everyone who had ever offended her. When they returned, I prayed for her, and God healed her instantly. Immediately, the pain disappeared, and she was able to move her fingers.

Why Should We Forgive?

Therefore the kingdom of heaven is like a certain king who wanted to settle accounts with his servants. And when he had begun to settle accounts, one was brought to him who owed him ten thousand talents. But as he was not able to pay, his master commanded that he be sold, with his wife and children and all that he had, and that payment be made. The servant therefore fell down before him, saying, 'Master, have patience with me, and I will pay you all.' Then the master of that servant was moved with compassion, released him, and forgave him the debt. **MATTHEW 18:23-27**

At that time, a talent was not currency, but it was equivalent to approximately 66 pounds of gold. So then, 10,000 talents would equal roughly 660,000 pounds; equivalent to 300 tons of gold. Today this comes close to 6 billion dollars. That's the debt that the king pardoned his servant.

With this illustration, Jesus exposed His point clearly to help us understand the magnitude of His love and forgiveness. He forgave you and me billions of dollars worth of sin. Let me put it another way: Suppose you are 50 years old and had knowledge of sin when you were 15. Let us also suppose that for 35 years you were such a wonderful person that you only committed one sin per day (365 per year). This would mean that right now you have 12,775 recorded sins committed against God. Now remember, we are only saying that you committed one sin per day, which is practically impossible.

In essence, Jesus said the servant owed a multibillion-dollar debt, and yet the king forgave him. In this illustration, the king is Jesus and the servant is the believer. Many Christians live as if God had only forgiven them $10 worth of debts. What makes people want to continue practicing sin? Why do they try to justify themselves when they do it? Why don't people appreciate the Kingdom of God or want to serve in it? Why are so many abandoning the Lord? Can anyone explain to me why people look for excuses not to attend church or why they are so ungrateful knowing they have been forgiven of so much? The answer to these questions is: because they regard their debt to be small and easy to forgive.

In my experience praying for the sick, I have found that many people suffer with arthritis. When I lay hands on them, the Lord reveals to me that the root of their condition is unforgiveness. When they repent and forgive after I pray for them, the Lord heals them instantly; this happens because repentance takes away the enemy's legal right to torment them.

> Forgiveness opens the door to our healing.

Now let us pray and seek God's forgiveness for keeping record of offenses and wrongdoings. Please repeat after me: "Holy Spirit, show me the areas in my life where I have unforgiveness, and give me the grace to forgive. I ask this in the name of our Lord, Jesus Christ. Lord, at this time, I renounce all bitterness and resentment. Today, I choose to forgive everyone who hurt me or caused me pain. I forgive them the same way God forgave me. In the powerful name of Jesus, I also forgive those who hurt me. I believe that You forgive me today. Therefore, I receive Your forgiveness by faith. I renounce every spirit of unforgiveness and cast it out of my life; in the name of Jesus. Amen!"

Testimony: Since she was a child, Yadira was mistreated by her family. The abuse led her to use drugs at a very early age. She drank heavily and suffered frequent episodes of depression. She even tried several times to take her life. She visited the church during one of our Thursday night services. She testifies that during the worship, the Lord spoke, telling her to forgive her mother. She knelt where she was standing and forgave her mother with all her heart. The Lord set her free, instantly. Today, she is a new person. She no longer drinks, uses drugs, or suffers with depression.

5. **Having some type of participation in the occult.**

Another obstacle that can keep us from our healing is the occult. Having anything to do with divination, playing the Ouija board, reading the horoscope, practicing witchcraft or masonry; doing yoga, visiting mediums, and palm reading are examples of participating in the occult. Getting involved with any of these practices will create a big obstacle to receiving our healing. These are like shadows that come upon people and become an impediment that keeps them from receiving their healing. Other ways in which the occult can manifest are Rock music and drugs. Satanic rock music has a strong demonic power, and if we expose ourselves to it, we will need deliverance.

You shall not bow down to their gods, nor serve them, nor do according to their works; but you shall utterly overthrow

them and completely break down their sacred pillars.
EXODUS 23:24

This warning was made by Moses to God's people; it was also accompanied by the promise that if they obeyed, they would reap great blessings (the blessings also belong to those who break away from the occult).

Testimony: Juan Carlos had suffered with asthma for 30 years. In efforts to feel better, he sought out the services of a Santero (Santeria), but nothing happened. During one of our many healing and miracles crusades, he received instant healing. God's power is greater that any occult practice.

Testimony: Marilyn practiced witchcraft. When she started to attend the church, her husband forced her to choose between God and him, and she chose God; he abandoned her, leaving her with nothing. She cried out to the Lord, and in only a few days she received a check for $4,000 she did not expect. From that day, God has met her every need.

At this time, I will ask you that if you have, in any way, shape, or form practiced the occult in any of the areas mentioned, please repent right now. Ask God to forgive you and pray the following prayer aloud: *"Lord, I was involved in the occult. Although I practiced it out of ignorance, I confess it as a sin and renounce it. I ask you to forgive me. I will never again involve myself in such practices. I renounce every spirit having to do with the occult, witchcraft, and divination. I rebuke them in the name of Jesus. From this moment forward, I am free. Amen!"*

6. Alliances with idol-worshippers

You shall make no covenant with them, nor with their gods.
EXODUS 23:32

Another obstacle that can keep us from our healing is allying ourselves with idol-worshippers or with their gods. Doing this makes us partakers of their sin and eventually become like them. Their gods become our gods, and we become like them. One such alliance is masonry. If you are still bound to this alliance, there is a curse lingering over your life. Even if you didn't practice it directly but your family did, you need to be ministered deliverance from that type of idolatry because it falls under the direct influence of a generational curse.

Masonry is a false religion; most of its ceremonies are demonic in nature, regardless of what its followers declare. Masonry practices idol-worshipping in combination to worshipping God. Any religious entity that combines their worship to idols and God is an abomination to Him, regardless of who practices it. The consequences are fatal.

Testimony: Four years ago, a lady visited our church. For 14 years she had practiced masonry but came to us seeking the peace she was unable to find there. She had believed that was the right path because of the Bible-reading sessions, but when she realized these sessions were only geared towards finding material blessings, she left. She knew the covenants they made were satanic; once she understood this, she came to church and was totally delivered. She is now a mentor, a House of Peace leader, and she travels the nations offering her medical services.

If you have ever been involved in masonry, repeat the following prayer out loud, *"Lord, I want to serve and love You. If there is any alliance in my life or in the lives of my loved ones having to do with the curse of masonry and the occult, I ask You to deliver me right now. I break its power in my life in the name of Jesus. Amen."*

7. **The effects of being under a generational curse**

Another obstacle that keeps us from receiving our healing is a generational curse; this is a deviation or sin committed by our ancestors. It is much like a black shadow or invisible hand from the past that comes back to interfere in the life of its intended victim, and keep him or her from accomplishing the desired goals; a generational curse is a constant source of frustration caused by the impossibility to succeed. If Jesus redeemed us from the curse, why are so many believers still under its influence? The answer is because some still refuse to accept or believe in the veracity of generational curses. However, believe it or not, they are real and can't be avoided, at least not humanly speaking. Jesus paid the price at the Cross to deliver us from them. If these did not exist, Jesus would have paid a high price at the Cross in vain. We must grab a hold of the complete work at the Cross because He paid for something that is real and can cause real damage.

Common indications of the existence of a curse:

- **Mental or emotional breakdowns.** Because of my experience in ministering to people with depression, I feel confident in saying that people who suffer depression, for prolonged periods of time, are indicative of a generational curse operating in their lives.

- Chronic illnesses. Chronic illnesses are evidence of the existence of a curse, especially if the condition runs in the family; for example, the grandmother, mother, daughter, and other members of the family suffer the same condition.

- **Continuous miscarriages and/or abortions.** Vaginal problems in women, including unpredictable menstrual flow, cancer, chronic bleeding, sterility, and cysts disappear when the curse is broken. Also, women who are able to get pregnant but whose baby dies during pregnancy (while still in the womb) are under a generation curse.

- **Divorces, separations, and the destruction of the family.** Divorce and adultery are destructive. When these are recurring within the same family, the curse cannot be broken in human strength, regardless of how much effort is put forth by the couple.

Testimony: A born again young man living in Nicaragua strayed from the Lord after he started to consume drugs and alcohol. When he entered the United States, he continued drinking and felt the need to return to the drugs. His situation caused him to lose everything, even his family. He tried to take his life on two occasions, once with a gun and the other by taking 15 pills. Praise God he was unsuccessful. His mother was a committed member of our church and would lovingly intercede for him. One day, she found him on the floor of her house. She began telling him that Jesus loved him and declared healing and deliverance over his life. He began throwing up and continued to do so all day. The next morning when he woke up, he felt sickened and revolted by the mere mention of drugs and alcohol. From that day, his life was transformed, and he started to attend church. Today, he is completely free and enjoying his new life.

Testimony: There was a young lady who was addicted to drugs, sex, gangs, and crime from the age of nine. At 17, she received Jesus as her Lord in one of our healing crusades. She had entered that lifestyle because of her father's influence and people in her life who practiced that type of lifestyle. Now she loves life and lives it for Him; singing rap music only for the Lord.

Now that we understand what generational curses can do, it is important to break and end their destructive path from our bloodline. At this time, I would like to guide you in a prayer to break them. Please repeat after me:

"Lord Jesus, I thank You for dying for me and for paying for the curse, sin, sickness, and poverty that held me in bondage. Right now, I assume responsibility for the sins of my ancestors. I recognize them and ask You to forgive me. I renounce every curse of mental and nervous breakdowns, emotional illnesses, marital tragedies, poverty, and sickness inherited through my blood line. Thank you, Lord, because You became a curse on the Cross to redeem me from it. Thank you because your sacrifice allowed the blessings to come into my life. Today, I loosen myself from any generational curse, and I declare my family and myself free from it. I claim the blessings promised to me at the Cross. In the name of Jesus. Amen."

Personal Testimony: There was a curse of sickness in my bloodline from my father's side. My grandfather and father both died from heart complications. When my father died, I started to feel pain in my chest. That curse wanted to pass into my life, but the instant I felt it, I rebuked the devil and broke the curse. This was approximately five to six years ago. A short time ago, I had my routine medical checkup, and the doctor told me that my heart was in perfect condition—healthy and without signs of any inherited heart disease. The curse was broken, and I live in total divine health. My constant prayer is that no one in my family, including my sons, dies of heart problems because my bloodline is redeemed from that curse.

Often, when I pray for the sick, I discern that the cause of their condition is demonic; hence, healing often includes rebuking demons. When Jesus prayed for the sick and rebuked demons, everyone was healed.

> When the sun was setting, all those who had any that were sick with various diseases brought them to Him; and He laid His hands on every one of them and healed them. And demons also came out of many, crying out and saying, 'You are the Christ the Son of God!' And He, rebuking them, did not allow them to speak, for they knew that He was the Christ. **LUKE 4:40, 41**

Rebuking demons is linked with the laying of hands. When the supernatural power of God manifests, the wicked spirits cannot resist and have to flee.

Two Common Ways to Demonstrate that Demons are Associated with Sickness

1. Demons are the indirect cause of sickness.

For example, when someone is oppressed, obsessed, or depressed by demons in the food area, as in the spirit of gluttony, the spirit forces that person to eat without measure. As a result, the person gains weight and is diagnosed with diabetes, which is a hereditary curse waiting to take over. This is what I refer to when I say a demon is the indirect cause of a sickness.

2. Demons are the direct cause of sickness.

In my experience, I have proven that 80% of all illnesses originate in the spirit realm or are produced by direct demonic influence. The common spirits involved are: pain, paralysis, sickness, and death. Many people have a curvature of the spine, as in scoliosis, which is caused by a spirit of paralysis that seeks to incapacitate or cripple the person, preventing him or her from receiving healing. For that person to be healed, the spirit causing it must be rebuked.

Testimony: In a healing crusade at church, a little girl came forward with juvenile diabetes. She had to inject herself with insulin for the rest of her life (there is no cure for this disease). After I prayed for her, she ate something in order to confirm her healing—prior to this, her sugar level would drastically rise after ingesting any type of food. After she ate, her sugar level was measured and the result was 81; she was completely normal.

The spirit of death weakens people, causing them to die before their time. These people tend to have a dark perspective of life. They often use dark and strange clothing and usually speak things such as: "I want to die. I am tired. Life is not worth living." These words are a clear invitation to the spirit of death and they are the worse type of confession anyone can declare.

I shall not die, but live, and declare the works of the LORD.
PSALM 118:17

You are being given an opportunity to take back the negative statements you have been declaring throughout your life and a good time to confess God's Word. If you are not instantly healed after removing these obstacles from your life, don't worry because many times healing is progressive.

They will take up serpents; and if they drink anything deadly, it will by no means hurt them; they will lay hands on the sick, and they will recover. **MARK 16:18**

Testimony: Orlando came from California to visit our church. He had suffered an accident in which he broke his back in three parts. The doctors were unsure if he would survive. He was undergoing therapy three times a day but was not able to bend over. When he came to church, he was in great pain, but the Lord healed him completely. Today, he is doing all the things he used to do before the accident. This miracle took place a little over a year ago.

You can receive your healing today of any sickness in your body or be free of any demonic oppression in your mind, emotions, or will. Join me in repeating the following prayer. As you read it, the Holy Spirit will touch your mind and life:

"Heavenly Father, in the name of Jesus, I rebuke the spirits of death, anxiety, fear, and depression. I order them to leave my mind, my emotions, and my will, right now. I rebuke every spirit of infirmity, sickness, and disease trying to oppress me. I declare myself healed and free according to Your promises found in Your Word. Amen."

Review

The obstacles to receiving healing are not placed by God but by our own actions. Jesus died on the Cross and was raised from the dead to give us power over all of Satan's work. The most common obstacles are:

- Ignorance: the enemy looks for open doors in order to enter our lives, especially in the areas where we have little or no understanding of God's truths.

- Doubt: this sin closes the door and keeps God's power from reaching us.

- Sin not confessed: this obstacle stops prosperity in any area of our lives.

- Unforgiveness: it paralyses the answers to our prayers.

- The occult, including divination, horoscopes, witchcraft, masonry, palm reading, and more will keep us from receiving our healing.

- Idol worshipping: Alliances with idol-worshippers and the worship of their gods will cause us to sin against God.

- Curses: Generational curses or curses inherited through our bloodline give Satan the legal right to operate in our lives.

I will now guide you in a prayer through which you will declare life instead of death. Repeat after me: "I will not die. I will live to share God's works. I choose life and reject death. I choose blessings and reject curses. I declare that I am healed from the top of my head to the soles of my feet; in the name of Jesus. Amen!"

Note:
To pray with Apostle Guillermo Maldonado and receive his powerful impartation, visit: kingjesus.org/jesus-heals-prayer

CHAPTER V

DELIVERANCE FROM UNBELIEF

*O*ne of the biggest obstacles keeping believers from receiving the healing that God promises in His Word is unbelief. In my experience in ministering and praying for thousands of people, I have concluded that unbelief is the number one barrier between receiving a miracle and not. The spiritual side of man yearns for God and exercises his faith, while the flesh wants to take the easy way out. This contrast can lead to idol-worship and witchcraft—a deceiving way to get "easy" and instant solutions to one's problems. For some reason, it seems easier to believe in alternative solutions to our problems than to believe in God's supernatural power. This is due to our emotions, feelings, thoughts, and circumstances that often find a way to obscure God's plans. Nevertheless, we must overcome these and believe in the reality of miracles!

God hates unbelief because it causes you to see Him small compared to your situation; it impedes you from seeing His power and greatness. But when you think this way, you are basically telling God that you believe He has no integrity in regard to His promises. In essence, unbelief negates the greatness of God's power. Biblically, unbelief is a surefire way to fail in life. It is no wonder it is the most common obstacle keeping people from receiving their healing, deliverance, provision, and miracles. Other times, however, miracles are not received because of open doors in our lives due to a sinful lifestyle, thus allowing the enemy the liberty to oppress us. But usually the greatest reason for not receiving our miracles is unbelief.

Unbelief is the only biblical reason to fail in life.

What is unbelief?

The word *unbelief* comes from the Greek word *apistia* which means: unfaithfulness, faithless, and weakness of faith.[1] When we doubt God and His promises, we are in fact declaring that He is not worthy of being trusted. Jesus never rebuked His disciples when they tried to imitate Him, for wanting to walk on water, or for trying to heal the sick and cast out demons. He did, however, strongly rebuke them for their unbelief. Today, this is still the only reason for God to rebuke us, for there is no legitimate reason for us to doubt His faithfulness. He has never abandoned or shamed us. He has always kept His promises.

> *He answered him and said, 'O faithless generation, how long shall I be with you? How long shall I bear with you? Bring him to Me. [...] Immediately the father of the child cried out and said with tears, 'Lord, I believe; help my unbelief!'"*
> **MARK 9:19, 24**

You might be reading this now and thinking that you want to believe, but you can't seem to do so. You are not alone. This occurred even in Bible days with Jesus standing before the people! The Word of God identifies this deep-seated unbelief through the Greek word *apistia*: the inability to believe in something even when we desperately want to. This is also known as "the sin of unbelief" which we will study in more detail later. The Bible verse you just read teaches that Jesus rebuked the disciples because they were unable to rebuke a demon from a young person due to their *apistia* or unbelief. You also learned about a desperate father who wanted to

---

1   Blue Letter Bible. "Dictionary and Word Search for apistia Strong's 570)". Blue Letter Bible. 1996-2009. 31 Aug 2009. < http://www.blueletterbible.org/lang/lexicon/lexicon.cfm>

believe Jesus' word, but in his difficulty, he reached out to Jesus for help: *"...help my unbelief."* This happens because humanity itself has been trained to doubt, while divine nature always believes. So how can you resolve this conflict between your two natures? Stop relying on your ability to believe, and revert to the faith of God. For example, have you ever faced a situation in which God spoke a prophetic word into your spirit, telling you He will do something great in your life, in your ministry, in your children, or perhaps in your health, but you think it is too great and difficult to accomplish? That is precisely the moment in which you must cry out to God, "Lord, help my unbelief", so He can give you the grace to believe.

What is biblical unbelief?

Unbelief is much more than just the absence of faith, the Bible defines unbelief as a sin caused by an evil spirit. This spirit keeps us from believing, even when what we are trying to believe for is common and reasonable.

Two aspects that manifest unbelief:

1. The sin of unbelief

But the cowardly, unbelieving, abominable, murderers, sexually immoral, sorcerers, idolaters, and all liars shall have their part in the lake which burns with fire and brimstone, which is the second death. **REVELATION 21:8**

As noted, the *cowardly, unbelieving, abominable, murderers, sexually immoral, sorcerers, idolaters, and all liars* are counted to be in the same category of those who will not enter heaven; these sinners are destined to eternal damnation.

Beware, brethren, lest there be in any of you an evil heart of unbelief in departing from the living God; but exhort one another daily, while it is called 'Today,' lest any of you be hardened through the deceitfulness of sin. **HEBREWS 3:12, 13**

The author of the book of Hebrews narrates the fate of the Israelite nation for not believing and obeying the Lord. God gave them countless signs and miracles during their desert journey. He gave them water from the rock, their shoes never wore out (their sandals grew with their feet), and they were guided by a cloud by day and a pillar of fire by night. He healed their bodies, fed them, and manifested extraordinary miracles; and yet, they chose not to believe that God was faithful. The consequence of their unbelief was their inability to enter the Promised Land; it cost them their blessing and kept them from enjoying the miracles received during their journey.

So we see that they could not enter in because of unbelief. **HEBREWS 3:19**

The sin of unbelief produces two things;

- **Separation from God.** This takes place when people begin to doubt God, His Word, and His promises.

- **A cold heart.** Before our hearts grow cold, we have the opportunity to see and hear many things from God that should help our unbelief, as it happened to the Israelites in the desert. However, some, even after witnessing supernatural manifestations, still choose to grow cold and not believe. Basically, they are not allowing God to persuade them.

We must use extreme caution to keep away from falling as victims to the spirit of unbelief. We must be alert, so it does not blind us to the things God wants to do in us and through us.

Unfortunately, it has become a common occurrence to see Christians who once served God be seduced and enticed by sin; consequently, they fall, their hearts grow cold and they end up serving the world, completely separated from God. Let us look at a verse that mentions how the sinful nature becomes a deterrent to our faith and a barrier to God's promises, regardless of our heartfelt desire to believe.

Jesus said to him, 'If you can believe, all things are possible to him who believes.' 24Immediately the father of the child cried out and said with tears, 'Lord, I believe; help my unbelief!' **MARK 9:23, 24**

Have you ever heard anyone say, "I'm trying to believe, but I can't?" In other words, they are saying they want to believe in the gifts of deliverance and healing that Jesus has made available to us, but the sin of unbelief keeps them from enjoying these. When you feel this way, and want to believe for your healing, but something in you keeps you from doing it, nothing will change until you confess the sin of unbelief. This will allow you to exercise the faith you need to make your miracles a reality.

What happened to the young man in the previous verse? The young man's father was persuaded by Jesus' words. Although his unbelief was evident at first, he finally believed, and obeyed; the result was his son's deliverance.

2. Unbelief is a wicked spirit

Before anything else, we must first understand that unbelief is a sin that separates us from God—a wicked spirit enters our lives when we continuously practice the sin of unbelief; its goal is to control and dominate our lives, causing our hearts to grow cold until we are lost forever.

Most of us were trained to doubt; to only believe in what our natural senses ratify as real. We have learned to live by sight instead of by faith. We have all heard the famous saying, "I'll believe it when I see it." This is substituting faith with reason. But God's Kingdom establishes the opposite: "We walk by faith not by sight."

Testimony: A lady was abandoned by her husband; out of spite and hate, she began a relationship with a married man who, after five years, also left her. Her situation caused her to fall into a deep depression; she would take sleeping pills to help her through the night and other medication to help her wake up. She wanted to die. She didn't believe in anything except in the power of money, but in her desperate state, she began to seek God. In her efforts, she visited a Catholic church where she paid for eight mass services in honor to a saint. She went every day for seven days, but nothing changed. On a Sunday morning, before the last mass was to take place, she turned on her TV and heard me preach. By the gift of knowledge, the Lord used me to speak a word that changed her life. She quickly got out of bed and visited our church instead of going to the Catholic Church; there, she gave her life to Jesus. Today she is a changed woman. She no longer takes sleeping pills and is able to sleep in peace; the Lord transformed her life. She let go of her unbelief and now firmly believes in God's promises.

Another Greek word used for unbelief is *apeitheia*. This word is stronger than the previous one. Although its first meaning is to disobey or to be unfaithful, its root goes deeper. In biblical and spiritual terms, *apeitheia* means: to deliberately decide not to believe. In other words, it means to go against, to freely choose to disobey. This is evidence that a spirit of unbelief is deeply rooted and fully operational in one's life. A person with this type of unbelief decides not to believe God, even though he has the tangible and visible evidence that God and His promises are real. Similarly, the Israelite people witnessed countless miracles never before known to man and yet, their hearts had grown cold, to the point of not believing God and refusing to heed His voice. Consequently, everyone above the age of 20, not counting women and children died in the desert (603,500 people, according to the military census registered in Exodus 38:26). Of that generation, only two entered the Promised Land.

Jesus' Disciples Were Blinded by Unbelief

Later He appeared to the eleven as they sat at the table; and He rebuked their unbelief and hardness of heart, because they did not believe those who had seen Him after He had risen. **MARK 16:14**

The disciples had the tangible evidence of Jesus' resurrection. He had told them seven times that He would be raised from the dead. On the morning, they went to the tomb, all they found was the sheet that had covered their Master's body. They had the physical, tangible evidence in their hands and still they did not believe. This goes beyond the sin of unbelief; it was a wicked spirit that kept them from understanding, seeing, or believing in His resurrection.

Many people have seen the wonders God has done in their lives and heard what He has done for others. Many have first-hand experience of God's power, healing their bodies, providing for their every need, performing financial miracles, keeping their children safe, delivering them from deadly accidents, giving them prophetic words, confirming their calling, revealing His plans for their lives and ministries and yet, they still doubt the source of their miracles or that God can do it again. This type of person is at risk of developing an evil heart full of unbelief.

If a spirit of unbelief is keeping you from believing and experiencing what God is doing in your life, then make a decision right now, and ask God to help you believe that He is your healer and that healing belongs to you because Jesus took your sickness upon Himself. He took your place and mine at the Cross. He died to take away our sin and our sickness. Believe that if we were created in God's likeness, and Heaven and Earth were created by Him, that Jesus paid the wages of our sins at the Cross and take away our sickness— the Word declares it! Sadly, people who are having the life drained from them by the spirit of unbelief are unable to see or understand this; they "feel" that the redeeming work of Jesus at the Cross is foolishness.

What type of people is attacked by the spirit of unbelief?

■ **People who live in a religious environment**

Throughout the years, I discovered that the spirit of unbelief is being released through the pulpit of many churches. This is especially true in churches where the leadership does not believe in using God's supernatural power and where healing and miracles are denied or simply ignored. These messages leave the people full of unbelief; hence, when they need a miracle from God, they are unable to receive it due to their lack of faith. This must sadden God greatly; to have the power to heal His people but be unable to do so because His own ministers close the door in His face only to open the door to the spirit of unbelief. Unbelief is a spirit, as is faith, and both are equally transferrable to people.

And since we have the same spirit of faith, according to what is written, 'I believed and therefore I spoke,' we also believe and therefore speak. **2 CORINTHIANS 4:13**

The spirit of faith, which comes from God, and the spirit of unbelief, which comes from the enemy, operate in the same realm and convince us of truth or lies, respectively.

With the spirit of faith, we are empowered to believe, regardless of what our natural senses dictate. With the spirit of unbelief, we refuse to believe regardless of what we see with our natural senses. Like many today, the Pharisees were being attacked by the spirits of unbelief and religiosity, disabling them from believing in Jesus even after witnessing the powerful miracles He performed. They preferred their traditions and religion over the redeeming work of Jesus; they refused to believe when He raised Lazarus from the dead and even tried to kill Him for it. Only those who are blinded by a demonic spirit could consider doing this!

Testimony: An apostle friend of mine, loved by many, shared the story of a Muslim woman who died and was resurrected by Jesus. When she told her story, she said that the moment her spirit left her body, descending into the valley of death, as told by the Scripture, Jesus suddenly appeared to her and said, "I am Jesus Christ. If you believe in me, I will resurrect you and restore your life." She responded, "I believe," even though no one had ever told her about Jesus. When she returned to her body, she found herself in her own wake surrounded by her loved ones. She opened her eyes, stood in front of them, and told them what she had just experienced. Her Muslim family, instead of rejoicing, went after her to kill her!

Now I ask you: How is it possible to witness a resurrection in the 21st Century, and not praise God for it? To instead get angry to the point of wanting to send that person back to their grave, simply because they are now professing a different religion than their own? That woman's family had experienced the visible and tangible evidence of her resurrection by the power of Jesus Christ; yet, were unable to believe. They were blinded by the spirit of unbelief due to their religiosity.

■ People who trust in their own intellect and mentality

I continuously encourage everyone in my congregation to study and graduate; to have a well-rounded education. I strongly believe that we can and must be amply educated and full of God, but I also believe we cannot trust in our own intellect or education alone. Our trust must come from God, not from anything created. We must surrender our minds and allow the Holy Spirit to guide and use our minds correctly.

> The educational system has replaced faith
> with reason and human wisdom.

The spirit of unbelief never acts alone; it always works in conjunction to the spirit of Greece, humanism, and intellectualism. Its characteristics are the following:

- It denies everything it cannot explain
- It denies the existence of the supernatural. It is common for this spirit to operate in places where the following biblical doctrines are denied:
  - miracles, signs, and wonders
  - the existence of demons and their expulsion
  - prophecy and the gifts of the Holy Spirit
- These spirits worship reason and human wisdom as if these were gods
- They veil people's minds and make them unable to see Jesus

  But their minds were blinded. For until this day the same veil remains unlifted in the reading of the Old Testament, because the veil is taken away in Christ. **2 CORINTHIANS 3:14**

- These spirits are directly responsible for not allowing people to receive their healing miracle

  And He marveled because of their unbelief. Then He went about the villages in a circuit, teaching. **MARK 6:6**

Do you come from a religious, traditional background? Does your background deny that miracles, healing, and the supernatural still take place? Do you trust and depend more on your intellect than in God? If your answers are affirmative, I now remind you that the intellect is the human ability to understand and reason, but God cannot be explained nor understood within the guidelines of human knowledge or reasoning. The only venues to know Him are by faith and by revelation of the Holy Spirit.

Personal Testimony: In the beginning, when God started to use me in miracles and healing, I would question everything because I wanted to understand how each physical miracle was taking place. One day I prayed for someone whose leg was shorter than the other and for another who had flat feet. After I prayed, the short leg grew before my eyes, becoming the same length as the other, and the flat feet got their curve. I was unable to explain this with my mind so I asked God. He taught me to do it by faith. He taught me there was no need to understand everything. We might not understand how a black cow can eat green grass and produce white milk, but we can believe God to give us our healing miracle. All we have to do is believe. Allow yourself to be persuaded and He will give you your miracle. Receive it! It doesn't matter if you understand it or not, just receive it!

How to be Free from the Spirit of Unbelief

If the spirit of unbelief is keeping you from admitting that God's promises are real and that they can be carried out in our lives, then you need to get rid of it. Do this immediately, the same way you would get rid of a poisonous snake in your vicinity. Therefore, if you don't want to grow cold and trade God's blessings for the deadly venom of the spirit of unbelief, this is what you must do:

- **Repent of the spirit of unbelief**

   Everyone must seek God and ask His forgiveness for doubting His word and promises. Likewise, you must repent for the sin of unbelief and renounce it from your life.

■ **Receive God's faith**

This is a powerful principle we learn from Scripture:

> Divine nature can only believe, it never doubts.
> Human nature cannot believe, it only doubts.

To believe God and His promises you must receive His nature; His eternal life. And to become true believers, you must live in its power. When I believe God's Word the same way He does, His Word in my lips has the same power as if it was spoken by Him. What is eternal life? It is the same type of life God has, and it was given to you and me the instant we received Jesus in our hearts. His Word teaches that he who has the Son has life.

Fight the good fight of faith, lay hold on eternal life, to which you were also called and have confessed the good confession in the presence of many witnesses. **1 TIMOTHY 6:12**

> Faith means to believe God's Word
> the same way God believes it.

The eternal life of God also has God's faith. Therefore, you must learn to grab a hold of eternal life.

So Jesus answered and said to them, 'Have faith in God.' **MARK 11:22**

A better way to restate this is, "To have the faith that belongs to God." Now repeat after me, out loud, *"Lord, I thank you for the eternal life You gave me through Jesus. This eternal life carries the faith that belongs to You and me. Right now, I receive it to believe the same way You believe. Amen!*

■ **Allow God to persuade you**

Unbelief is the freewill choice not to believe. Then, we can deduce that faith also implies the voluntary action to believe in God, His Word, and His promises. Perhaps we are in the same mental state as the father of the demonized son who said, "Lord, I want to believe; help my unbelief!" Regardless of how hard it is and even if you don't know how to, choose God and not the enemy. Once you do, the Holy Spirit will give you the grace to believe.

Personal Testimony: Many years ago, my friend and prophet, Hank Kunneman, revealed to me that God would use me to perform His miracles and healing in four types of individuals: the blind, mute, deaf, and lame. In the beginning, this was hard for me to believe. Being keenly aware of my own weaknesses, I decided to recognize before God my inability to do anything in my own strength. I said, "Lord, I choose to allow your Holy Spirit to persuade me, and I decide to move forward in faith and pray for those types of sicknesses." The following Sunday, I called forth all who were blind, deaf, mute, and lame. I prayed for them. The first time only two people were healed; the second time more people were healed. Since then I have witnessed numerous people who were blind, deaf, mute, and lame receive their healing. I am thoroughly convinced that our Lord Jesus did it all. It may have been an effort to believe at first, but praise God I allowed Him to persuade me and to heal His children through me.

Abraham Allowed God to Persuade Him

And being fully convinced that what He had promised He was also able to perform. **ROMANS 4:21**

The fact that Abraham allowed God to persuade and convict him does not mean he never doubted the promise; of course, he doubted! He not only doubted but he and his wife also laughed when the Lord told him His plans. After thinking it over, he decided to believe and obey God. Regardless of the circumstances, his age, and Sarah's sterility, He decided to believe God and allow himself to be persuaded.

Many people are struggling, trying to have enough faith to reach their miracle and healing, when in fact they will never be able to accomplish it with their human nature and in their own strength. Regardless of how you feel or what you understand, regardless of the circumstances, receive God's faith. Decide to believe and obey. Never choose against God; believe His word, believe in His promises, praise Him, and you will receive your miracle.

Review

God hates unbelief because it makes Him seem small and incompetent. Unbelief is one way to deny God's integrity in His Word and in the greatness of His power.

- Unbelief is the inability to believe regardless of how much we try

- Unbelief manifests as a sin and as a demonic spirit

- The spirit of unbelief attacks those who are living in a

religious environment and those who trust solely on their level of education, knowledge, and intellect

■ To be free from the spirit of unbelief, you must repent of this sin, receive God's faith, and allow yourself to be persuaded by Him

Some may need to repeat one or all of the following prayers:

"Father, I don't understand what is happening. What you are asking me to do is beyond my ability to comprehend. Everything seems to contradict what you say. My body feels the pain, my mind is in a state of confusion, I feel a deep sense of despair, and I am being attacked by fears and insecurity. However, I freely choose to allow you to persuade me. Holy Spirit, help my unbelief! I choose to obey God and His Word, and with His faith I receive my miracle, my healing, my provision, and my blessings right now. Amen!"

"Lord, I don't understand what is happening. What You are asking me to do is beyond my ability to comprehend, but I say to You right now: persuade me. Open up my heart and help me to choose prosperity instead of poverty; life and blessings instead of death and curses. In the name of Jesus, I declare myself prosperous and blessed. Amen!"

Prayer to Renounce the Spirit of Unbelief

The only way to rebuke and cast out the spirit of unbelief is for each person, of their own free will, to renounce it. Please repeat the following prayer out loud:

"Heavenly Father, please forgive me for allowing the spirit of unbelief, the spirit of humanism, and the spirit of Greece to enter my life. Right now I renounce every spirit that tries

to reason with your Word and the spirit of unbelief. I order them to leave right now, in the name of Jesus. Amen!"

Note:

To pray with Apostle Guillermo Maldonado and receive his powerful impartation, visit: kingjesus.org/jesus-heals-prayer

CHAPTER VI

BIBLICAL METHODS GOD USES TO HEAL

*W*e often pretend to understand God using natural rules, regulations, or logical reasoning. We even trust our methodology and formulas to try and explain Him, forgetting that God supersedes our limited understanding, imagination, and abilities.

During the time that God has gracefully given me to minister healing to thousands of people, I have found that some miss their miracle because they don't believe that God can heal them through a specific method. They approach the altar with a preconceived idea of how their healing miracle should take place, and when it does not happen as they hoped, they simply assume that God is not going to heal them. However, as we will learn in this chapter, God is not limited to just one way of doing things. To better understand this concept, this chapter will review the main methods God uses to heal—all of which are clearly stated in the Bible. In doing this, we will learn how to take ownership of our healing miracle which is rightfully ours. However, as we do this, we should be clear of the following: God is sovereign, and He can give you your miracle in a way other than how you might expect it will be. God can perform His miracles how, when, and where He pleases. Now, let us review eight of the most popular methods God uses to heal, as shown in Scriptures:

1. Laying of hands

The laying of hands is one fundamental method found in the doctrine of Jesus Chris; yet, most congregations fail to speak on the subject.

What is Laying of Hands?

The laying of hands is one way God uses to transfer divine virtue, blessings, authority, power, wisdom, healing, and deliverance to us. Its main function is to continue transferring generational blessings and inheritance to the Body of Christ from one ministry to another and from generation to generation. Furthermore, it is also one of the methods God uses to impart healing and miracles from one person to another!

Because the laying of hands method is also the most natural way to make physical contact between the people involved, the effects are felt by both the giver and the receiver of the miracle.

...They will lay hands on the sick, and they will recover.
MARK 16:18

When Jesus taught the disciples on the Great Commission, He commanded believers to lay hands on the sick in order to impart healing to them. In doing so, He delegated His power and authority over every believer; so that their hands could be God's instrument by which blessings and virtue would be imparted and transmitted to others. This is how we can give others what He has given us. The key word here is impartation.

What is Impartation?

The word *impartation* means the transference of anointing and power from one person to another by the laying of hands. When we do this, we are obeying the Great Commission and putting into action God's Word. Jesus first practiced and modeled this method and then commanded us to follow His example.

> *Then Jesus put out His hand and touched him, saying, 'I am willing; be cleansed.' Immediately his leprosy was cleansed.* **MATTHEW 8:3**

Testimony: One of my spiritual daughters suffered with intense migraines; these were so strong that getting out of bed was almost impossible to do, and the pain was so debilitating and blinding that she had to take prescription medication that kept her in a drugged state. When she was brought to my office, I placed my hand on her shoulder and rebuked the spirit of sickness that was causing that pain and instantly she was healed! This confirms that when I laid my hands on her, the power of God was imparted and healing became definite. Praise God, she was completely healed.

Testimony: In August 2006, a young man in our church named Andy was diagnosed with cancer in his left foot. He was to be operated on the following week, but his mother was not in agreement with the procedure the doctors expected to follow for his recovery—the operation was risky. The mother and son attended a service believing in God's power to heal. I prayed for him through the laying of hands, and the child fell backwards. He was on the floor for almost 10 minutes, as if in a state of unconsciousness. While I prayed for him, I felt as though he was pulling from within me. I made sure his mother knew there was something very special about her son. Later, she took her son to the hospital, seeking a second medical opinion. When the tests were redone, the doctors concluded that the child was completely healed. He was healed by the power of God that was flowing through my hands as I made contact with his body.

2. God's Word

Another Biblical method through which God heals is God's Word—the Bible. When I first started in the ministry of healing, I would only minister to a few people at a time during meetings and services. As the ministry grew, we went from small places to stadiums and open terrain because these venues enabled multitudes to receive at the same time. Accordingly, unlike when I minister or pray for people at a church service, it is merely impossible to lay hands on each person individually. Therefore, I must impart healing by a different method: through sending forth God's Word. This action requires a greater level of faith in me, but the Lord's support has been amazing.

- **The written Word:** When I verbally declare God's Word and speak it forth; it does what it is sent to do: heal.

- **The Rhema Word:** This word is directly spoken by God into our spirit, and it is meant to be used in a specific situation or moment. When a *Rhema* word is spoken and heard, people are automatically delivered and healed.

Jesus often spoke words of healing unto the people, for example:

- Jesus sent the word to the centurion's servant.

  Therefore I did not even think myself worthy to come to You. But say the word, and my servant will be healed.
  LUKE 7:7

  In this scenario, we learn that the Centurion's servant was healed without ever having to come into physical contact with Jesus. He simply spoke the word, and the servant was healed.

- The Word of the Lord is medicine to our bodies.

For they are life to those who find them, and health to all their flesh. **PROVERBS 4:22**

When we take ownership of His Word (logos) we receive physical healing. I have been able to prove the importance of speaking the healing Word to our bodies on a daily basis. Personally, I declare His Word to my internal organs, my mind, my spirit, my heart, my respiratory system, and my circulatory system every single day.

Many believe that being healed by God is the best that could happen to them; however, although this is a great thing indeed (thus the reason I wrote this book) there is an even better miracle than this: to live in divine health and never get sick. In order to have divine health it is utterly important to speak God's Word to our bodies, after all, Proverbs 4:22 states that it is medicine to our bodies.

Testimony: A lady visited our church because her mother in Cuba was severely sick, with her lungs nearly destroyed. That day, the lady received a healing impartation and a Word she could speak forth to her sick mother. Although her mother was far away, in another land, she was able to receive healing and today she is completely healed.

It is vital to understand that distance is not an obstacle to God's Word. In other words, when people are prayed for, they do not have to be physically present because the Word is spirit. Therefore, when it is sent by our spoken confession, the Bible promises it will do that which it is sent to do. Regardless of where one may be, His Word will never return void. It is a God-given promise. It will carry out the purpose for which it was sent. If you are sick, you can declare the Word of God to your body or someone else can do it for you; then, your corresponding action is to simply receive it, confess it, and believe it wholeheartedly! This means you must be convinced that His spoken Word has the power to heal your body and give you the opportunity to live fully and in divine health.

3. God heals through anointed objects

The third biblical method God uses to heal us is through anointed objects; this can be anything from a towel, a picture, clothing belonging to the sick person, or any other object that will come into contact with the person in need of healing. It is important to point out that these objects, whatever they might be, are not "good luck charms", for these objects in and of themselves have no power. Only Jesus has the power—He is the healer. The object only serves as a point of contact; as a transporter of the anointing; and as a means through which the sick person will be able to loosen his faith. However, it is solely through God's power that a godly miracle takes place because God's anointing is a heavenly substance that can accumulate in objects. When a sick person comes into contact with an anointed object, it will help to loosen the healing.

Now God worked unusual miracles by the hands of Paul, that even handkerchiefs or aprons were brought from his body to the sick, and the diseases left them and the evil spirits went out of them. **ACTS 19:11, 12**

122

In this verse, we learn that people were taking pieces of cloth from Paul's clothing and placing them on those who were sick. According to the original translation, Paul would cut off pieces of his clothing, which had come into contact with his body and which were anointed by the Holy Spirit, and distributed the pieces among the crowds. When the sick or demon-possessed would touch his clothing, they were instantly healed and delivered. Notice I added *delivered*; it is necessary to emphasize that each time someone is healed they are also being delivered from demonic activity or possession. In addition to healing the sick, the anointing in an object can also cast out demons.

Jesus' Clothing was Anointed

Now He could do no mighty work there, except that He laid His hands on a few sick people and healed them. And He marveled because of their unbelief. Then He went about the villages in a circuit, teaching. **MARK 6:5, 6**

Many people wanted to touch Jesus, as it happened with the woman with the issue of blood; here we see the pattern that was later repeated by Paul: The anointing was stored in Jesus' clothing because it was in constant contact with his anointed body; thus, everyone who touched it was delivered and healed!

Testimony: A renowned evangelist in the United States once shared a true story about a woman whose husband was an atheist. The woman approached him with a piece of candy and asked the evangelist to keep it in his pocket while he preached and then to return it to her after the service was over. The evangelist did not understand the reason for this but accepted to do it. He took the candy and held it in his pocket the entire time he preached. When the service was over, he returned it to the woman. She went home and gave the candy to her husband. As soon as he ate it, he was touched by the power of God which gave him the conviction that he needed Jesus; subsequently, he received Jesus as his Lord and Savior and was born again. God delivered that woman's husband from his spiritual blindness.

From this testimony, we also learn that we cannot impose upon God a specific method through which we can or should receive our miracle. God can use anything to carry out His will, as long as the faith of the person needing the miracle is on Jesus and not on the object.

God's anointing can be drenched on clothes and objects. Personally, I have often used this method and thus have heard countless testimonies on healing through the use of anointed towels. Usually, I lay hands on a towel, pray over it for the person in need, and then I anoint it with oil and loosen the anointing over it. Later, the towels are given to people in hospitals or in their homes and they receive their healing miracle right where they are. Many have been healed of cancer and other terminal illnesses. I always make sure that people understand that these objects are not good luck charms but objects that act as the channel or the point of contact for the sick person to loosen his faith. Healing and deliverance are just some of the wonders that occur when God's anointing becomes impregnated into an object.

Testimony: While ministering in a miracle crusade in San Pedro Sula, Honduras, a woman approached me. She was blind in one eye and the other was beginning to also deteriorate. The doctors had diagnosed that she would lose her sight completely. At the end of the crusade, I exited through the back and she was there waiting for me. As I walked out, she extended her hand and touched my jacket. She had faith and believed that if she could touch my coat, God's power would heal her. When she touched me, God healed her instantly. I had no idea what had taken place until she came to Miami to testify. She was healed! It is evident that I was not the one who healed her; it was God's anointing stored in my clothes that flowed into her body and gave her the healing she needed. She took a hold of her miracle by force!

4. Anoint with oil

Is anyone among you sick? Let him call for the elders of the church, and let them pray over him, anointing him with oil in the name of the Lord. **JAMES 5:14**

It is vitally important to understand that the Bible calls for the elders of a church to anoint and pray for the sick. An elder is an individual who has received God's authority to pray for the sick to be healed. For this to take place, a church's government must be well established. Interestingly enough, few churches practice this. I believe we must repent before God for not doing it because the Bible is clearly commanding us to practice this method amongst our churches. Especially because the responsibility of an elder is more spiritual in nature than administrative; elders are meant to pray for people's needs and by it cause deliverance, healing, and miracles to take place.

Why should we anoint with oil?

In the Old Testament, the oil for the holy anointing was made up of different ingredients and used to separate and

125

consecrate people unto ministry and service to God. In the Bible, oil is symbolic of the Holy Spirit. Oil, in and of itself, does not heal; but, the same principle concerning anointed objects applies here. The Holy Spirit heals.

Oil, like anointed objects, also serves as a point of contact for those who need healing. In this case, the elders should be doing the anointing; this is a widely used practice in our church. We have hundreds of elders who work together with me during the miracle crusades where I normally make an altar call for anyone who needs healing, and I ask the elders to anoint with oil the people who come forward. They pray for the sick and many are healed and delivered.

Testimony: Not long ago, a sister in Christ lost a child and had another being treated for depression. The young man saw me on television and received Jesus as his Lord and Savior; he was recovering from a drug overdose for which he asked God and his mother for forgiveness. When I heard what had happened, he was still bedridden and in the process of recovery. I anointed a small towel with oil, declared God's word and His power over it, and sent it to him. When the mother placed the towel on her son, God's power broke the power of sin, drug and alcohol addiction. He was completely set free.

So far you have learned that Jesus heals through the laying of hands, anointed objects, the spoken Word, and through the anointing with oil by the elders of a church, but there is more...

5. **God also heals through the gifts of the Holy Spirit.**

Among the gifts of the Holy Spirit, there are a few specifically designated to produce healing. These gifts of power that operate in the body of Christ are labeled in the Bible as: the gift of healing, the gift of miracles, and the gift of faith. Please keep in mind that in saying this I am not implying that the other gifts cannot bring healing, deliverance, or a miracle. Before defining each gift, let us be fully clear on what defines miracles and if they still exist.

Do miracles still exist?

- **Jesus began His public ministry with miracles.**

...His fame went throughout all Syria; and they brought to Him all sick people who were afflicted with various diseases and torments, and those who were demon-possessed, epileptics, and paralytics; and He healed them.
MATTHEW 4:24

Jesus' conception and birth, His life and wisdom, His teachings and ministry, His death and resurrection, His reappearance and ascension, are all undeniably powerful miracles themselves. Likewise, when His Church was established, it also began with miracles.

...Lord, look on their threats, and grant to Your servants that with all boldness they may speak Your word, by stretching out Your hand to heal, and that signs and wonders may be done through the name of Your Holy Servant Jesus.
ACTS 4:29, 30

When the first Christians realized that Jesus had resurrected from death and that in His name they were able to administer His same power to perform the same miracles He had performed, a river of miracles emerged. This flow of the miraculous, through the first apostles' hands, enraged the religious leadership and inevitably shook their government's foundation.

Christianity began in the midst of this shaking. Miracles were their defining mark, distinguishing the primitive church from others. In the book of Acts we read of the first accounts of the Christian church which include many miraculous accounts, none of which are ever implied to cease from reoccurring. Without the supernatural, Christianity is only a religion, like any other ritual, sect, or human philosophy. Biblical Christianity is much more than a religious entity; it is life (religion is a dogma; a creed, a formality, a ceremony to be kept and observed repeatedly). Christianity is life. It is something that excites the heart. The nature of Jesus manifested this life when He walked among us. Christianity began with a miracle. Its foundation lies on a series of them. Miracles have and continue to be the leading evangelical tool to widespread Christianity. Furthermore, the Bible itself is a book of miraculous accounts; a divine registry of every event that took place from the beginning of time. In fact, even before Christianity, many men and prophets mentioned in the Old Testament witnessed miracles in response to their faith.

What is the purpose for the miracles that took place in the Old Testament?

The purpose for the miracles has always been to help the people understand that there is a vast difference between the dead gods and the one and only living God; Creator of heaven and earth. Regardless of the time in which miracles took place, they served the same purpose they continue to serve today: to persuade unbelievers into shifting their minds and beliefs to worshiping the Lord.

Sadly, in the Old Testament, when the miracles ended, the people would return to idol-worshipping until it was time for them to seek a new series of miracles. Mankind needs a living God because it passionately seeks the miraculous. That is why people find someone who is usually surrounded by great multitudes and whose prayers are heard and answered by God; this person does not have to be a philosopher or a famous politician because people are seeking miracles not individuals.

What is the deepest desire of man?

Man was created to live in the supernatural. This is why Jesus did not stop Peter from walking on water because he was created for that reason: to live in the supernatural. Furthermore, the purpose and plan for humanity, from the beginning, was to have the supernatural ability and authority to exercise dominion and lordship over the natural realm and to be able to move in the supernatural one. For man is not made of flesh and bones alone; rather, we are spirits, who have souls, that live in a body. Adam and Eve were created in God's image and likeness and were placed in the Garden of Eden to carry out God's plan for His creation. Since we were created in His image, we will never be satisfied without Him. Our innate instinct is to seek Him and to find the essence of who we are in Him, for this is our true identity.

Every individual has the intrinsic hunger to experience the supernatural and miraculous. Secular education will never completely eliminate that thirst or hunger; it only suppresses it. Some may affirm that education has replaced miracles, that we no longer need the supernatural to manifest God's existence, love, and glory. However, the truth is that people want to know a real God. This is why every revival that has taken place has always been accompanied by the manifestation of the supernatural. Whenever and wherever the Word of God is welcomed, believed, and acted upon accordingly, the miraculous becomes evident. All men cry out for the supernatural power; they yearn for tangible demonstrations of God's power. Even philosophers, agnostics, Gnostics, scientists, and atheists want to experience miracles.

The desire for the miraculous is deeply rooted in the heart of man, regardless of color, race, gender, or nationality. Mankind is the result of a miracle of God. When Jesus walked amongst us, the people cried out for miracles. Today, over 2,000 years later, the same cry can be heard. Jesus is the same miracle-maker today as when He lived among us, the only difference being that He now lives in heaven, where He exercises His authority so we can manifest His miracles. The Bible is clear when it teaches us that Jesus does not change.

Jesus Christ is the same yesterday, today, and forever. **Hebrews 13:8**

Through us, Jesus has and will manifest the real essence of Christianity which cannot be experienced in rituals, creeds, dogmas, or man-made ceremonies but only in the manifested supernatural power of His glory.

- **Jesus' miracles attracted the masses.**

Then a great multitude followed Him, because they saw His signs which He performed on those who were diseased. **JOHN 6:2**

Today, multitudes are drawn to wherever miracles are produced in the name of Jesus. I have proven this in every nation I have had the privilege to share His Word. These massive audiences have had the opportunity to experience God's supernatural power.

Why does our faith seem to fail when it comes to miracles?

When people are taught about financial prosperity, the response is impressive; they quickly demonstrate the level of faith needed to receive their financial breakthrough. However, many traditions have become rooted in the body of Christ that caused counterproductive teachings resulting in doubt and unbelief when it comes to the miraculous; the end result being the inability to believe in miracles.

...Making the word of God of no effect through your tradition which you have handed down. And many such things you do. **MARK 7:13**

Theology without the supernatural cannot produce biblical results. Christians who only preach the philosophies of an obsolete theology will never win men for Christ. Rather, we need to plant seeds of faith. God's Word, accompanied by miracles, will produce faith in the hearts of those who hear it and see it. Only then will we achieve greater results in our lives and ministries.

Now the parable is this: The seed is the word of God. **LUKE 8:11**

Sick people will be healed and unbelievers will turn to Christ every time and everywhere the biblical Gospel on healing and miracles is proclaimed with the corresponding actions.

What is my personal experience concerning miracles?

I have been blessed with the opportunity to minister healing and miracles in over 46 countries across the globe.

During this time, I have proven that the greatest miracles received have come after hearing God's Word and taking a corresponding action, by faith. In truth, I have only laid hands on people very few times. This is clearly indicative that speaking forth God's Word in regard to healing and miracles produces in people the faith necessary to receive their miracle.

Why the emphasis and urgency for miracles?

Now when He was in Jerusalem at the Passover, during the feast, many believed in His name when they saw the signs which He did. **JOHN 2:23**

The manifestation of miracles helps people believe in the Gospel of Jesus Christ; hence, it is no wonder that when Jesus walked the Earth, He proclaimed God's Kingdom and confirmed what He preached through miracles. The Bible teaches that He was approved by the great miracles He performed.

Men of Israel, hear these words: Jesus of Nazareth, a Man attested by God to you by miracles, wonders, and signs which God did through Him in your midst, as you yourselves also know. **ACTS 2:22**

According to the book of Acts, by following Jesus example, the disciples caused the primitive church to prosper. Today, the need for miracles is as urgent as it was in those days. Thankfully, Jesus promised that if we believed in Him, we would do the same and even greater works than He did, today!

Most assuredly, I say to you, he who believes in Me, the works that I do he will do also; and greater works than these he will do, because I go to My Father. **JOHN 14:12**

What is the conclusion?

The conclusion is that God is who He says He is; that we are who He says we are; that He has what He says He has; that we have what He says we have; that God does what He says He will do; and that we will do everything He says we will do. The entire Body of Christ is called to manifest miracles and healing because He continues to be its Miracle-Maker. Jesus has not changed. He continues to be the same in the twenty-first century and everywhere in the world.

This introduction on miracles was extremely important to make because it introduces the three gifts that operate in miraculous healing. Allow me to clarify once more that the aforementioned are not the only gifts, for God often gives us a different gift, if necessary, to lead someone to their unique healing miracle.

What exactly does it mean to receive a physical healing?

A physical healing occurs when an organ is restored or recovered to its normal state; it can take place instantly or progressively.

133

...They will take up serpents; and if they drink anything deadly, it will by no means hurt them; they will lay hands on the sick, and they will recover. MARK **16:18**

A Spanish translation of the above verse explicitly says the sick will recover or be restored. Also, a healing is considered to have taken place when the activity causing the illness stops operating in the body. When that influence is uprooted, the person receives total healing. Healing occurs in one of two ways:

- Instantly
- Progressively

...When He saw them, He said to them, "Go, show yourselves to the priests." And so it was that as they went, they were cleansed. LUKE **17:14**

This verse is indicative that the lepers were not healed instantly; they received their miracle as they went to see the priest to testify they were healed. We cannot impose our ideas upon God as to how we should receive our healing or miracle. All we can and should do is believe we will receive—at any given moment—our miracle or physical healing, whether it's instant or not. Moreover, thanking God even before the miracle takes place and being willing to share our testimony of it are key attitudes of a miracle recipient.

What is a creative miracle?

A creative miracle takes place when God creates a new organ or part of a damaged organ; also, when He produces something that was not previously there. For the most part, this type of miracle is instantaneous.

Today, many have witnessed that God's miracles are not confined to the physical body. He is performing all types of other miracles: emotional, financial, family, relationships, and more. Often, when I am praying for people, God shows me what types of healing miracles need to take place. When this occurs, it means that the gifts of *word of knowledge* and the *gift of miracle and healing* are happening simultaneously.

Testimony: While ministering in my church, God gave me the specific name of a man in the service with his specific condition; he had heart and bone problems. God wanted to heal him. When I called his name, he came forward using crutches. He was the only one who came forward, and he was sitting in the center isle three rows from the front. I ordered his heart to be healed and his feet to be restored, in Jesus name. Instantly, he let go of the crutches (he had used these for several years) and started to walk normally. The Lord revealed his name and the condition he was in through the gift of the word of knowledge, and He healed him through the gift of healing.

God can do the miracle. He is the same. He never changes. Now, all you must do is grab a hold of this truth! Regardless of what you need, God can and wants to do it. All you have to do is to stretch your faith and He will deliver you.

Testimony: At the end of one of our Sunday services, the Holy Spirit spoke the name of a woman. He revealed that she had been suffering with intense chronic back pain for the past three years. The doctors were unable to discover the cause or the answer to help her. Through the gift of the word of knowledge, God gave me her name, the condition she was in, and even allowed me to feel her pain in my own back. Instead of ending the service, I called the woman, by her name, and asked her to come forth to the altar. Only one lady approached the altar, she was the one. I prayed for her and her pain instantly left her. That same day, she returned to our evening service to testify that God had healed her. As one can see, this was another example of how the gift of the word of knowledge and the gift of healing worked together to produce her miracle.

6. God heals through praise and worship.

On countless occasions, people have received their healing while they were praising and worshiping God in a service. God's presence descended and healed them. It is important for God's people to be educated in the power of praise and worship because the moment we receive the revelation of what it truly means, its effects and what it can do against the enemy, we will see God's glory manifest in our lives.

What is praise?

Praise is our declaration to God of who He is and of His powerful works; it is expressed through music, dance, applause, shouts of jubilee, and through various bodily postures.

What is worship?

To worship is to have an attitude of humility, reverence, and of respect for God expressed through bodily postures such as kneeling, hands raised, heads inclined, or falling prostrate before His presence. Worship is also God's answer to our praise. Although there is much to discuss

136

on this topic, as I do in my book *Ascending in Prayer and Worship and Descending in Warfare*, I will go over some basic principles on praise and worship that will help you pave the way to your miracle.

Most people think of praise as a time for fast songs, and worship as a time for slow emotional songs, but these definitions are wrong. Rather, praise is when we ascend into God's presence, and worship is when God descends to have communion with us. No one can enter His presence without praise and giving him thanks because only our praise and the blood of Jesus can grant us access to our Father's presence. In other words, praise is initiated by us, but worship is an attitude given by the Holy Spirit that creates within us a spirit of genuine worship; hence, we are able to worship the Father in spirit and in truth. We are talking about more than singing or playing musical instruments; it is a heartfelt attitude that expresses our fear of the Lord—our reverence toward Him. When we combine both praise and worship, a spiritual atmosphere is produced where God's power is able to descend and heal, deliver, save, and perform any type of creative miracle.

Testimony: While preaching in Maracaibo, Venezuela, I was surprised by a miracle that took place due to someone's holy persistence. That someone is a lady who had traveled to the United States on the basis of faith—she had heard from God that if I prayed for her she would be healed. Unfortunately, when she got to Miami, I was away on vacation. So she tried again, this time she came to meet me during a recording I was doing as host for TBN's *Praise the Lord*, but again, she missed me because I left before she could reach me. Relentless, when she heard that I would be traveling to Maracaibo, she gave it one more shot and flew to Venezuela. After seven hours of travel, she was in bad shape. Finally we met. She was in a wheelchair unable to speak due to her condition. The cancer had spread throughout her body, including her brain. I asked her husband to take her to the healing crusade where God would heal her. During the worship time at the crusade, I started to preach about praise and worship. I had not prayed for anyone yet when suddenly, that lady who had been wheeled in by her husband got on her feet and started to walk and speak normally! This was a result of the people's passionate praise and worship and His glory descending. In the midst of this glorious atmosphere the lady was completely healed, instantly.

God is looking for that type of atmosphere in our meetings, churches, and home. When we worship God in spirit and in truth, we will receive our healing and every other blessing God has for us. Many people seek their miracle in many ways but fail to praise and worship Him. If you are one of those people and nothing has worked, begin to praise until the spirit of worship descends; then worship until God's glory descends and heals your body and gives you the miracle you are desperately seeking.

7. **God heals when we take the Lord's Supper**

...And when He had given thanks, He broke it and said, "Take, eat; this is My body which is broken for you; do this in remembrance of Me." **1 CORINTHIANS 11:24**

In this verse, the word remembrance means to actively remember something we consider to be meaningful. Thus, we continually remember what Jesus did on the Cross, including His death, resurrection, and return. If we take the Lord's Supper with this understanding, then it becomes a powerful spiritual moment that will produce the perfect atmosphere in which we can receive our healing. However, if we take it as a simple religious act, without respect or the full revelation of its observance, there will be less than favorable consequences. Many believe that taking the Lord's Supper is a religious activity in which we take the bread and wine and carry out a ritual, but that is far from it. Taking the Lord's Supper is done in memory of Jesus and His sacrifice. It has great power to heal and deliver.

What does it mean to take the Lord's Supper in an unworthy manner?

Therefore whoever eats this bread or drinks this cup of the Lord in an unworthy manner will be guilty of the body and blood of the Lord. But let a man examine himself, and so let him eat of the bread and drink of the cup. For he who eats and drinks in an unworthy manner eats and drinks judgment to himself, not discerning the Lord's body. For this reason many are weak and sick among you, and many sleep.
1 CORINTHIANS 11:27-30

These verses teach that many have become sick and others have died as a consequence to taking the Lord's Supper in an unworthy manner. On the other hand, this also means that if we take it with the right attitude, we will see miracles take place.

Taking the Lord's Supper with reverence and in a manner worthy of receiving its blessings instead of its judgment, we cannot be living in sin or in contention with others. If we acknowledge that we have been living sinfully but still wish to receive of its blessing and be cleansed of our sin, then we must do the following: prior to eating the bread and wine—representing His body and blood—ask God to forgive your sins, then commit to living in holiness. Otherwise, those who eat and drink of it unworthily, while living in sin, will eat and drink judgment rather than blessing. Therefore, if we need healing, strength, revelation, and deliverance, let us partake of the Lord's Supper with reverence, respect, and understanding.

Testimony: A lady diagnosed with a thyroid problem felt the power of God descend and fell to the floor after taking the Lord's Supper during one of our services. During her experience, she felt that something was being taken or pulled from her thyroid gland. Today, she is healed. Praise God!

8. God heals by faith and the prayers of others.

Confess your trespasses to one another, and pray for one another, that you may be healed. The effective, fervent prayer of a righteous man avails much. **JAMES 5:16**

Some people's faith is underdeveloped or newly acquired; hence, they need others to stand in the gap and exercise their faith for them to help them believe.

When Jesus saw their faith, He said to the paralytic, 'Son, your sins are forgiven you.' **MARK 2:5**

The individuals mentioned in this verse had the faith to lower the sick man through the roof, providing the perfect moment for Jesus to work in their favor. When Jesus saw their faith and their corresponding action to that faith, He healed him. Note that it was not the sick man's faith that healed him; it was his friends'. Likewise, most often it is the parents' faith that provides their children's healing or vice versa. If you believe that Jesus has the power and continues to produce miracles, He will heal you or the person you are praying for.

Testimony: During a miracle crusade in Nicaragua, I met a mother who had traveled several hours to take her nine-year-old daughter, who was deaf since birth, to the crusade. When she testified on the platform, she said her daughter had written on a piece of paper that she would be healed if she attended the crusade. The mother acted by faith, believed, and took her daughter to the crusade. When I prayed for the sick, the little girl was in the front praying, believing, praising God, and appropriating her healing. On that day, she spoke and heard for the first time in nine years. God opened her ears and loosened her tongue through her faith and her mother's corresponding action.

Let us recap: God can heal through the laying of hands, His Word, anointed objects, the anointing of oil, the gifts of the Holy Spirit, praise and worship, the Lord's Supper, and by the faith and prayer of others.

How do we receive our miracle or healing?

To receive our miracle, we must first understand the following three things:

■ **God wants**

...A leper came and worshiped Him, saying, 'Lord, if You are willing, You can make me clean.' Then Jesus put out His

hand and touched him, saying, 'I am willing; be cleansed.'
Immediately his leprosy was cleansed. **MATTHEW 8:2, 3**

God is powerful to intervene in our lives and produce a miracle, and best of all He wants to do it because we are His children. The sign that proves He wants to perform miracles and healing out of love for you and I is what Jesus did at the Cross of Calvary: Jesus died for our sins. When Jesus said, "I am willing," He was expressing His perfect will for us. He does not want us to suffer with sickness or without peace and joy. He wants us healed! Do not doubt that it is His will. His desire to give us our miracle is greater than our desire for it. Yet, many have a paradox belief of God's love: they believe that God can heal them, but He simply does not want to—this could not be further from the truth.

But Jesus looked at them and said, "With men it is impossible, but not with God; for with God all things are possible." **MARK 10:27**

Everything includes *everything*. God is omnipotent to do beyond what we ask or understand. Whatever you need, God can do. He can work in any situation and nothing is impossible for Him.

■ **God is ready**

Yes, God wants, can, and His power is ready to deliver, heal, save, and perform any miracle and healing to benefit us; the only thing left for us to do is learn to receive it. Remember, God is ready!

...And the power of the Lord was present to heal them. **LUKE 5:17**

Oftentimes, God's power manifests itself but it is rejected by atmospheres saturated with tradition or doubt; however, this does not negate the fact that God's power is ready to rescue us.

Receiving Our Miracle, Today

Jesus said to him, 'If you can believe, all things are possible to him who believes.' **MARK 9:23**

Everything is possible to those who believe wholeheartedly. Regardless of the doctor's diagnosis or the circumstances, if you believe, everything is possible. Are you ready to receive your healing? Are you ready for your miracle? Let me remind you that God wants, can, and is ready to heal you right now.

Review

■ Although the Bible highlights eight methods through which God performs healing miracles, we know that He is sovereign and can do so in any way He chooses.

■ The laying of hands is one way to impart healing because it activates the law of contact through which divine virtue is transferred from one person to the other, thus a miracle takes place.

■ God's Word—whether it's written (logos) or Rhema (A word spoken by God and impressed in our spirit)—given by the Holy Spirit for a specific case and time, activates His power to heal.

■ When we speak God's Word to our bodies it has the power to heal and provide divine health for a lifetime. The miracle of divine health is even greater than the miracle of healing.

■ Anointed objects are used by God to heal because the

anointing is a substance that is stored in our bodies, clothing, and in objects.

■ The anointing with oil, used since the beginning of time, is symbolic of the Holy Spirit, and it operates by God's power. The elders of the church are called to anoint the sick with oil and pray for their healing.

■ The gifts of the Holy Spirit are a channel used to impart divine healing, especially the gifts of power which are: the gift of healing, the gift of miracles, and the gift of faith.

■ In the Old Testament, miracles were a means to identify the one true God; thus, eliminating the pagan and dead gods and motivating the people to return to the Lord. The same is happening today.

■ Man's inborn desire is to live and experience the supernatural. Consequently, if we lack the faith to believe in miracles it is due to the lack of proper teaching concerning God's power.

■ A physical healing is the instantaneous or progressive restoration of an organ in the body that was deteriorated.

■ Praise and worship are the venues through which God's healing flows into our lives and bodies. Praise is the proclamation of who God is and of His powerful deeds expressed through music, songs, and shouts. Worship is the humble attitude, reverence, and respect we give God expressed by different bodily postures including: raising our hands, kneeling, bowing our heads, or laying prostrate before the Lord; this produces a spiritual atmosphere in which God's power can flow and heal.

■ The Lord's Supper was established by Jesus in remembrance of His death and resurrection; two events that changed our history. Each time we partake of it in a worthy manner, we receive His power that heals, delivers, and strengthens us.

- The faith and prayers of others represent the eighth method through which God heals those who have insufficient faith to receive their miracle.

- God wants, God can, and God is ready to heal us; all we have left to do is appropriate ourselves of the miracle by faith, and it is done.

- All things are possible to those who believe.

In what do we base our faith: the Word, our pain, or the devil?

We must decide whom we are going to believe. God's Word declares that we are healed; pain declares that the illness is present, and the devil declares that we are sick. However, we do not walk by our senses. Therefore, when we feel the pain, we must believe God's Word has already worked its good will in us; walking by faith, not by what we feel. The method God wants to use to heal us is not important; what is important is to be open to receive it. Allow me to pray for you right now through this book:

Heavenly Father, thank you because everyone reading this book has the faith to believe that God can, wants, and is ready to heal them. They will not pay attention to the symptoms or the devil's voice whispering in their ears; they will listen and believe Your Word which is greater. They believe in Jesus, the miracle maker, who never changes. As they read this prayer, they are touched, transformed, and healed by Your supernatural power, right now. Those in need of a healing miracle, receive it right now. For those who need a creative miracle in their bodies I pray right now, in

God's power, for that organ, bone, ears, eyes, kidney, or any other part of their body to be restored. If an organ in their bodies has deteriorated, I declare it is restored like new. I speak God's Word and declare you healed and set them free of the disease. If you are being oppressed in your mind or heart with evil thoughts, depression, or death I declare you free, right now! Thank you, Jesus. Amen!

Note:

To pray with Apostle Guillermo Maldonado and receive his powerful impartation, visit: kingjesus.org/jesus-heals-prayer

CHAPTER VII

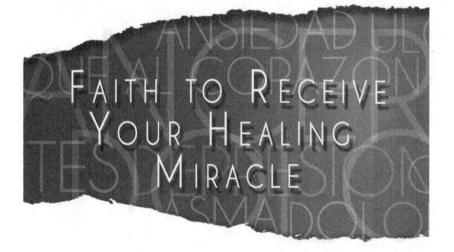

FAITH TO RECEIVE
YOUR HEALING
MIRACLE

*F*aith continues to be a popular topic among Christians and even secular circles—even if many of them have little to no biblical understanding of what it is and how it works. The understanding of biblical faith was recently restored to the Christian church a few decades ago. Sadly, each time God restores a truth to the Body of Christ, the enemy raises false argumentation in an attempt to discredit it. This struggle between lie and truth has often caused people of faith to take the doctrine to an extreme, to the point of bondage. For example, when the Faith Movement began it was indeed a genuine movement with a genuine revelation received by Prophet Kenneth Hagen; nonetheless, many took it to an extreme. They went beyond the level of faith and entered into what may be known as "super faith" or simply put: presumptuousness. Therefore, in this chapter we will study the true revelation of faith and the proper way to apply it.

Why is it so important to live by faith?

> *Behold the proud, His soul is not upright in him; but the just shall live by his faith.* **HABAKKUK 2:4**

The phrase *shall live*, in this verse, comes from the Greek word *chayah*, which means to enjoy life or live happily. The definition goes even further than that, it also means to flourish; exist; breathe; to be of good cheer; to recover one's health and to live without hindrances; be saved; sleep, eat, prosper, worship, work, tithe, and give offerings. Basically, the main idea produced by the word *chayah* is concentrated in two verbs: live and breathe. Therefore, what this verse is really saying, according to the Hebraic culture is that if we choose to live without faith, we are not living at all. Faith is the element that gives us the strength to overcome difficulties, problems, crisis, and adversity. When we exercise our faith, we bear the evidence of the life that is within us; we are implicitly telling the world that we have not and will not give up. *Chayah* includes every dimension of human personality and experience, in every aspect imaginable, including: spiritual, mental, physical, and material. The simple act of eating recognizes that God has provided the nourishment. In other words, everything that we do is by faith because we acknowledge that life is a privilege that only derives from God.

But he who doubts is condemned if he eats, because he does not eat from faith; for whatever is not from faith is sin. **ROMANS 14:23**

Anything we do without faith is considered sin. Simply stated, if we do anything out of fear, envy, hate, bitterness, or to satisfy our ego, we will not be approved by God because it is impossible to please Him without faith.

Failure is inevitable when we choose
to depend on ourselves.

But without faith it is impossible to please Him, for he who comes to God must believe that He is, and that He is a rewarder of those who diligently seek Him. **HEBREWS 11:6**

Also, we must do everything in love, patience, mercy, and justice, this includes our prayers and when giving our tithes and offerings. How can we expect for God to approve our deeds when we do them without faith? Hence, we must be fully convinced that living by faith is a necessity, not only to please God but also to receive everything He has for us—the complete package He left us at the Cross of Calvary. It is only when we live by faith that we can receive our healing miracle.

...Faith is the substance of things hoped for, the evidence of things not seen. **HEBREWS 11:1**

Two Lifestyles

There are two lifestyles one can choose to practice:

1. Live by sight.

For we walk by faith, not by sight. **2 CORINTHIANS 5:7**

What does it mean to live by sight? It means that we are guided by our natural senses; what we see, hear, smell, touch, or taste. When we walk by sight we are totally depending on our own capabilities and feelings; in doing so we exercise our own will instead of God's will for our lives. This is exactly what happened to Adam: he chose to live independent from God and dependent on himself; in other words, he chose to live by sight.

2. Live by faith.

Another way to describe this lifestyle is: "The righteous lives by faith, not according to his natural senses." He is not guided by what he sees or hears, but by what the natural senses are incapable of perceiving. Needless to say, this lifestyle makes us completely dependent on God. This is why God wants us to walk by faith and not by sight. If we understand that faith is the channel through which we will please God, then it is vital that we learn what it means and how to live by it.

Dear friend, are you among those who often say, "I'll believe it when I see it?" Are you ill and still dare to say, "I don't believe in miracles or believe that Jesus heals today." Let me ask you another question: Can you heal yourself? Then, it is worth giving faith a try.

Testimony: Two years ago, a lady was diagnosed with intraocular pressure, causing her to suffer optic nerve damage and an eventual total loss of vision. Her condition began with a tickling sensation in the eye. A year later, she was totally blind in her left eye. When this happened, her right eye had to work harder. According to the doctor, she would eventually lose sight in her right eye and there was no hope of recovery. The doctor also said that an operation could cause her to lose her sight faster. When I prayed for her, I rebuked the spirit of blindness. She received the word, placed her hand over her left eye, and received her healing by faith. Today she has perfect vision in both eyes.

Faith is not...

Within Christian and secular circles, among evangelicals and non-believers, and even in world religions, most people believe they have faith, but they don't; consequently, they become frustrated and progressively worse when the miracle or healing they need never takes place.

Illustration: A person once asked me, "Pastor, why did an illness take my mom's life if she was a woman of faith?" My answer was, "If your mother was a woman of faith but died, rest upon the fact that she was saved, therefore she received eternal life."

> Faith allows us to receive from
> God that which we lack.

Before defining the word faith, we must first understand that faith is not any of the following five things:

1. Faith is not magical.

If your lifestyle is void of faith, don't expect to live by faith from one moment to the next. Many feels that faith will suddenly appear as if by magic. They think that their health issue will disappear simply by stating that they have faith. This is not so because faith is like a muscle, it must be exercised and developed progressively. As we exercise our faith for the small things, we will learn to believe for greater things.

Personally, when I decided to live by faith, I started to exercise it with the little things. For example: believing God that I would quickly find a parking space at the supermarket or mall. Immediately after I prayed, someone would drive away leaving me their parking spot. Eventually, I started to pray for the sick, starting with the "small" illnesses such as a headache. As time passed and I saw my prayers being answered, my faith progressively developed to believe for healing for those who had chronic or life-threatening illnesses.

2. Faith is not an emergency kit.

The time to exercise your faith is before you get sick, not after the enemy attacks your body. If you do, you will not be caught by surprise and you will be amply prepared to deal with any situation. Many Christians want to use their faith the same way they use spare tires, when the emergency presents itself. Faith is clearly one of the most important virtues, but it must be progressively developed.

Therefore, as people of faith—righteous people—we are to exercise faith as a lifestyle, and not merely as an emergency kit.

Illustration: I have probably used the spare tire in my car a total of four or five times. When I used it the first time, I had no idea how to raise the car and change the tire. I was overwhelmed. I had to get someone to help me. I lacked the experience to do it properly; hence, when the problem arose, I had no idea how to handle it. In short, if we fail to exercise our faith, we will not know how to activate it when we need a miracle, when a crisis hits, when we lose our job, or when we get sick. Faith, like our muscles, must be exercised and developed! If you recognize that you have been using faith like an emergency kit or believe it is like magic, you must change the way you think because faith is a lifestyle.

3. **Faith is *not* knowledge.**

Knowledge is a relative—a cousin—of faith. When we judge anything based on its proven existence or by our natural senses (sight, touch, smell, feel, and hearing), we are operating by knowledge, not by faith.

4. **Faith is not hope.**

Hope and faith go hand in hand but are not synonymous. The difference between hope and faith is that hope has no substance, it cannot be perceived; whereas, faith is the tangible, concrete, and substance of what we hope for (Heb 11:1). Furthermore, if a believer claims to have faith but has no hope, his faith is void. Faith is the undeniable, firm assurance of the reality of (the things unseen and those we hope for) to be concrete and tangible now. Hope lies in the future, but faith is received today. God can send the believer dreams and visions, but if the believer lacks faith these become surreal ideas that will never materialize. Hope stirs our faith, but faith makes our hope materialize.

I have prayed for many sick people and declared them healed in the name of Jesus; yet, when someone asked them, "How do you feel?" They answered, "I feel fine. I know I will be healed." Did you notice the implication of their words? Their answer speaks of hoping to be healed, not knowing that they are healed. Therefore, they are not. Hope is like a helping hand that gives us the green light to receive, but our faith doesn't stop there, it receives. Both work together, but only faith will make our promises attainable. Hence, we must shift from hope to faith.

5. **Faith is not presumptuous.**

It is important to note that many Christians are living in a state of presumptuousness instead of faith. In saying that some are presumptuous, I am referring to those who believe they have faith, but in truth, they are trying to believe in something that is beyond their level of understanding.

Illustration: Some people have shared with me their plan of buying a $200,000 house, which would render a mortgage of $2,000, having a monthly income of only $1,500. They claim they want to buy it "by faith" and ask what I think on the matter. I call this presumptuousness. Perhaps someone can pay that house, but these people did not have the budget to do so. Although God has given us faith, and living by faith is always risky because we are acting on conviction and trusting in what we do not see, He has also given us common sense.

To briefly summarize the important points learned so far, we know that faith is vitally important because doubt is sin that brings condemnation and separates us from God's blessings. While we are in our earthly bodies, we can only live one of two ways: by sight or by faith. To live by sight means to depend on our five natural senses, but to live by faith is to depend totally on God and trust even if we do not see. Faith is not a magic potion or an emergency kit; it is not knowledge, hope, or presumptuousness. Faith is not for tomorrow, it is for today!

Testimony: After seven months of attending our church, a lady asked for prayer. She had been unable to conceive for years because she was missing one fallopian tube. So, I prayed for her. Six months later, she was six months pregnant and came to the altar to publicly testify of her creative miracle! The doctor was unable to explain to her how her complete reproductive system had been restored and recreated. Today she is constantly reminded of her wonderful miracle by the precious smile on her baby's face.

What is faith?

Now faith is the substance of things hoped for, the evidence of things not seen. **HEBREWS 11:1**

Now let us carefully study three key words in relation to faith. If you have decided you want to live by faith and understand that this is a prerequisite to receiving God's blessings, to please Him, and to live with hope, strength, and joy; then, you must also have a clear-cut understanding of the following: how it works, how it is loosened, and just how we are supposed to live by it. Let us break down Hebrews 11:1:

■ **"Now, faith is…"**

Faith is a now thing; it is not for the future. It is in the present tense: faith *is*. Knowing this leads to the understanding that God is the Great I am, not the Great "I was"; the One who dwells in eternity, in the ever-constant present. It is important to understand that faith is related to eternity and that it is God's dwelling place—God is eternal! Eternity, contrary to popular belief, is referring to a permanent state of being; much like the marital status of an individual, not a long period of time. In this eternal state, everything is: Healing, deliverance, and life are a done deal—they simply are. Therefore, through our faith we have access to the dimension of eternity, also known as "the dimension of glory" or "God's dwelling place." Eternity is a spiritual realm. Therefore, faith gives us access to everything that exists in eternity and brings it forth into the physical realm; hence, faith is.

■ **"…the substance of things hoped for…"**

The Greek word for substance is *hypostasis*, meaning: trust, substance, assurance, or title deed. It is a legal term that was used in civil courts when a set of documents established property ownership. Likewise today, when you are the bearer of a title deed, you know the piece of land stipulated in that document belongs to you even if you have not seen the property yet.

Illustration: Some time ago we purchased 16 blocks of land in Honduras to build an orphanage. I sent my brother the money to buy the land. He took care of the legal transactions and when it was ready, he sent me a copy of the title deed. This was sufficient for me to know and guarantee that the church owned the land. Although I had never seen the property, the title deed and all the legal documentation I had describing the land was proof of our ownership. How can we apply this to our personal life? Later I will explain this in greater detail.

■ **"...the evidence of things not seen..."**

The Greek word for evidence is *elegchos*, which means: conviction, persuasion, evidence, irrefutable proof or certainty of something we have yet to see. This is also a legal term, but it is mostly used in criminal courts. This is the type of evidence that convinces the jury of the guilt or innocence of a defendant, and it produces the same effect as if the jury had been physically present in the scene of the crime and witnessed the entire scene with their own eyes. This *evidence* gives the jury the impression of having witnessed the crime when in fact, they were never anywhere near the site—the evidence causes them to see.

If we join the three words defining faith, we could say that faith is the assurance of the reality of tangible things that we have yet to physically see but that do exist in the spiritual realm. By definition, what we wait and hope for cannot be visible in the natural realm because if it is, we no longer believe by faith but by sight. Faith is based on something real, not in dreams or fantasies. Faith believes for invisible things; that which cannot be physically seen but is still real because it exists in the realm, dimension, atmosphere, or state of being of eternity. Initially, we may not be able to see, hear, or touch these things with our physical senses, but we can materialize them by faith. Similarly, it is impossible to obtain a genuine title deed if the property is non-existent. It is impossible to obtain concrete and convincing proof of a crime that never took place. Accordingly, the fact that we have the title deed or the convincing proof of the existence of what we are hoping for is guarantee enough of its authenticity, even before we lay our eyes on it.

All of our blessings already exist in eternity, in the spirit realm. We just have to bring them into the physical realm. God spoke them into existence in the spiritual realm and they are greater than any material matter, precisely because they are eternal.

> ...While we do not look at the things which are seen, but at the things which are not seen. For the things which are seen are temporary, but the things which are not seen are eternal. **2 CORINTHIANS 4:18**

The purpose of faith is to take that which exists in the spirit realm and manifest it in this world's time and space. Faith has the power to penetrate the eternal realm of the spirit and take what God created with His Word. Faith brings forth our blessings so that through faith these things could be seen and experienced in this world. All things are first created by God in the spirit realm by His voice or Word; thus, the things that once were not suddenly are.

> ('...I have made you a father of many nations') in the presence of Him whom he believed—God, who gives life to the dead and calls those things which do not exist as though they did. **ROMANS 4:17**

God usually speaks things into being in the spirit realm; then He waits for faith to be exercised in order to manifest them in the material world. If we try to manifest anything in the material realm that does not exist in the spirit realm, it is a presumption on our part and not faith. How can you apply this to your life? Do you need a miracle for your body? Do you need a new kidney or for an organ to be restored? I have good news for you. That kidney or organ you need is waiting for you in the dimension of eternity—God's dimension of glory. Do you see it? It already exists in the spirit realm! Many call this realm the fourth dimension, but if we use Biblical terms, it is the dimension of eternity or glory. Therefore, if you need a miracle, take ownership of it by faith that you may receive it in this world. Remember, God has spoken: His Word says that He blessed us with every spiritual blessing in the heavenly places.

> Faith cannot create; it can only obtain. Only God's word can create something from nothing. Faith can only obtain what His word has already created.

Blessed be the God and Father of our Lord Jesus Christ, who has blessed us with every spiritual blessing in the heavenly places in Christ. **EPHESIANS 1:3**

Your blessings await you. As God's child, all you have to do is make them yours. Now is the time to receive them because faith is not for the future, it is for today. Do you want to know where you can find the title deed of your blessing? What guarantee do you have that what you need is waiting for you? What guarantees your healing, deliverance, or the restoration of your family and home? How can you be sure that God can deliver you from a drug addiction, depression, or crisis? The answer to all your questions is: God's Word.

...His divine power has given to us all things that pertain to life and godliness, through the knowledge of Him who called us by glory and virtue, by which have been given to us exceedingly great and precious promises, that through these you may be partakers of the divine nature... **2 PETER 1:3, 4**

God's Word contains over 30,000 promises of what God has already created and waits for us in the spirit realm. His Word is the title deed that guarantees their existence. For example, if you are sick, 1 Peter 2:24 is the title deed required to obtain your healing...

...Who Himself bore our sins in His own body on the tree, that we, having died to sins, might live for righteousness—by whose stripes you were healed. **1 PETER 2:24**

If God said it in His Word, it is a done deal; that is the title deed He has given us to guarantee our healing. Perhaps some of you are still wondering whether your miracle is already in existence, but this is exactly where faith plays a vital part; if you believe it though you do not yet see it, the miracle is yours.

Testimony: The Holy Spirit gave me a word of science by which I knew that a specific woman had cysts and that He was healing her at that moment. The woman happened to be serving in the evangelistic ministry. When she heard her name being called, she did not hesitate to go forward and take ownership of God's spoken word and receive her miracle. She had suffered four years with this condition. The pain was almost unbearable and she had to take pain killers to get through each day. When she went forward, she felt like her body was on fire. When she visited the doctor, she was told there was a void where the cysts used to be. The Lord removed them and healed her.

Do all believers have faith?

*...Not to think of himself more highly than he ought to think,
but to think soberly, as God has dealt to each one a measure
of faith.* **ROMANS 12:3**

> It is in man's nature to doubt because he
> lacks the faith to believe. Divine nature
> always believes; it never doubts.

God gave everyone who has received Jesus as their Lord and
Savior a measure of faith. Why? Because we cannot create
faith to believe in God and His Word; we can only receive it
from Him. He wrote His Word and has the faith to believe
it. He doesn't just wake up one day and doubt in His own
promises. God is a faith God, and His children must learn to
live by faith. Who are His children? His children are those
who invite Jesus to be their Lord and Savior. Remember, we
cannot produce faith, it is given to us, and Jesus is the author
and finisher of our faith.

So Jesus answered and said to them, 'Have faith in God.'
MARK 11:22

A more precise translation (WYC) says, "*...have ye the faith of
God...*" This makes a lot of sense because if we have the same
faith as God, we can believe His Word in the same way He
does. God has given us a measure of faith to grow and use it.
He is a good investor, and He will not give anyone a greater
measure of faith if he is not going to use it. Therefore, let us
use the measure of faith God has given to us to believe in Him
and in His Word. We must work with God's faith because our
innate human nature is to doubt.

I have been crucified with Christ; it is no longer I who live, but Christ lives in me; and the life which I now live in the flesh I live by faith in the Son of God, who loved me and gave Himself for me. **GALATIANS 2:20**

In this verse, Paul affirms that before Christ's arrival he had no faith, but he allowed the Son of God to demonstrate His faith through him. What we must do is reach out and receive His faith. If we feel unable to do so, then we should ask the Lord for help to believe in His Word in the same way that He believes it. Do this now and receive His faith now, in the name of Jesus!

Two sources that will help us receive and develop our faith:

■ **The written Word**

The main source of our faith is the written Word; it is developed as we dare to see and hear the things that we desire.

This only I want to learn from you: Did you receive the Spirit by the works of the law, or by the hearing of faith? [...] Therefore He who supplies the Spirit to you and works miracles among you, does He do it by the works of the law, or by the hearing of faith? **GALATIANS 3:2, 5**

■ **A Rhema word or a word spoken by God into our spirit.**

So then faith comes by hearing, and hearing by the word of God. **ROMANS 10:17**

Rhema is a word given by God at a specific moment; it is impressed in our spirit and vivified by the Holy Spirit. It doesn't necessarily come by reading the Word—although it is important to read it—for faith comes through hearing the Word of God. It can be spoken by God directly into our spirit or we can find it in the Bible. If we hear it with faith, the word will grow in us and help us believe and receive what God has for us. An important detail we should never forget is that Rhema never contradicts the written Word. God will never give us a Word that contradicts a principle established by Him. He never contradicts Himself; never!

Testimony: A married couple was trying to conceive for ten years. They tried everything to no avail. In one of our services, I said that God had revealed there were women in the congregation unable to conceive, and asked them to come forward to the altar. A woman came forward, believing the specific word given by God at that moment (Rhema), and a year later she came forward again, this time to present her two-month old son before the Lord and the congregation. Two years prior to this wonderful moment, she had entered into a covenant with God and was awaiting her harvest. The doctor that took care of her during her pregnancy was the same one that was going to treat her for infertility. Needless to say, the doctor was amazed by the miracle. When the couple gave their testimony, the woman said her miracle could only have been produced by God. According to her doctor, this was one of the best pregnancies she had overseen in many years.

How do we loosen our faith?

Faith is loosened by our confession. Let us break down the word confession: It comes from the Greek words *homologeo* or *homou*, which means: being together; of persons assembled together; and logos which means: a word, the sayings of God, or a thought, declaration, a weighty saying, a dictum, or maxim.1 In other words, the word confession means to say the same thing as another or to agree with someone else and declare the same words. If we want the blessings God established for us in the eternal realm to Cross over into the physical realm, we must align our words with God's Word—His will and declarations for us.

Illustration: Some time ago, one of my toes was causing me great pain. The doctor told me it was Gout produced by stress or perhaps bad eating habits as a result from an overload of uric acid in the body. Upon hearing this, I went before the Lord and declared the following: "I order the pain in my toe to leave. I speak to it right now and order it to be healed. It is done in the spirit realm and in eternity; therefore, I declare myself healed. I order the uric acid accumulated in my body to dry up right now." Every morning, I would continue to say, "Thank you, Lord, because I am healed. Thank you because I believe the uric acid dried up." Two or three days later, my toe was perfectly healed. One of the doctors in my church examined me and said that it was impossible for the toe to have dried up because when the liquid accumulates it must come out, and when it does it is a sticky substance. However, my toe was perfectly normal and dry as a direct result of my declaration of faith. The example I am trying to give with this testimony is that I used my words to order the sickness to leave, and I asked God to heal me. I took my healing from the spirit realm, brought it into the physical realm, and it manifested in my body. If you are sick, begin to confess your healing. Stop declaring negative confessions because the power of life and death is in your tongue (Proverbs 18:21).

How do we take faith-filled actions?

Thus also faith by itself, if it does not have works, is dead. But someone will say, 'You have faith, and I have works.' Show me your faith without your works, and I will show you my faith by my works. **JAMES 2:17, 18**

The Word of God is full of examples showing the difference between works and faith. In order to live by faith, it is important to understand the source of our faith, what faith is not, how to loosen it through our confession, and finally, we must learn to take faith-filled actions. Basically, it means that we ought to take the corresponding action according to what we are confessing and believing. James reminds us that Abraham believed and took action. When God told him to take his only son, Isaac, and offer him up as a living sacrifice, he did his part and obeyed. It is not enough to confess, we must also take the corresponding action.

In every healing crusade, after I pray for the sick, the demon possessed, and those in need of deliverance, I always tell them to take a corresponding action; in other words, to do something they could not do before (i.e. move their hands, bend over, stand, etc.). This often results in many that were once bound to a wheelchair to stand up and walk after I say, "Stand up and walk!"

God has given us many prophetic words, but those words demand that we take a corresponding action. Maybe the Lord has already revealed to you your specific calling. Are you preparing yourself for it? Are you taking the corresponding action(s)? Has God told you that you would own and operate an international business? Have you established the corporation to launch this new venture?

As I am writing this I feel that God is speaking to many of you right now.

It is not just a matter of talking about it, although this too is part of the process. It is also a matter of having God's faith to be healed. God gave us of His faith so we could believe for our healing. If we try to use our own faith, we will certainly fail because we are incapable of doing so in and of ourselves. We need His faith to take our blessings from eternity and manifest them in the natural realm.

Up to now we have learned that faith believes for now and hope believes for the future. Faith is certainty; it is the title deed of what belongs to us even though we cannot see it. Faith is the conviction we have; the undisputable proof that we have that which we cannot see; it is the evidence that places us in the scene without physically being there. Remember, faith does not create; it obtains. Everyone is given a measure of faith to believe, and it will grow as we exercise and develop it. We now know that the written Word and Rhema are two venues through which God speaks to our spirit. Faith is loosened by our confession and it is vivified through our corresponding actions.

Testimony: A 12-year-old child had suffered with ulcerative colitis since the age of seven. This disease is the chronic inflammation of the large intestine, causing ulcers and inflammation of the inner lining of the colon, abdominal pain, diarrhea, and rectal bleeding. Nicole came to the church in excruciating pain. After I prayed for her, she felt heat cover her body—this was the power of God embracing her entire body and making her pain-free. She was instantly healed and enjoying life today without that horrible illness.

The Prayer of Faith

> *...the prayer of faith will save the sick, and the Lord will raise him up. And if he has committed sins, he will be forgiven.*
> **JAMES 5:15**

The prayer of faith will never do its job if the individual has any doubt if it is God's will to heal him. If you are still wondering and doubting God's will, don't expect to receive anything. Don't even bother declaring the prayer of faith. Please know this: You don't have to suffer any longer. God's will is to heal you!

How does the prayer of faith work?

Some people believe that the proof of their prayer being heard is that the answer has to come immediately; but this is not always so. Sadly, many miss their blessings, their healing, their miracles or deliverance because they try dictating to God just how and when God should do it. Confessing a prayer of faith doesn't automatically mean the answer will be received immediately. Rather, we must simply declare it believing in the Word and in what God has promised He will do. Your blessings are there for the taking, and your title deed is God's promise to you (You find it in His Word) which guarantees they will come to pass. For example, if you want the salvation of your family, go to the Bible and seek the title deed of your property of salvation which is: "...You and all your household will be saved." Acts 11:14. Your salvation and that of your family is already in the spirit realm, in the realm of glory. All you have to do is take it.

Faith vs. Symptoms

You can verbally declare your healing through confessing a prayer of faith. But if you do it just "hoping", your prayer will sound something like this, "I will be healed. I hope God heals me." You must declare it with faith and say, "In the name of Jesus, I am healed!" This is faith; even if the symptoms persist, faith declares that you are healed because God's Word says you are. The title deed God gave you—His promises—say you are. Faith is not afraid to stand on the Word. The devil might remind you of the symptoms—"It still hurts!"—but you will declare with confidence, "I am healed. God healed me!"

Testimony: A lady was diagnosed with Myasthenia Gravis; a chronic autoimmune neuromuscular disease causing weakness of the muscles. In the most extreme cases, the muscles are completely paralyzed causing death by asphyxiation. She was bedridden and living in Nicaragua. When she saw me through our TV program, Tiempo de Cambio (A Time for Change), she heard me say, "Rise up." She appropriated the word and stood up. She is now completely healed and able to move and do what she could not do before.

Faith and Our Five Senses

While the Word enhances your faith, it drowns out your senses for they are incompatible with it. Remember that walking by sight means to use the natural senses, not faith. Therefore, faith must ignore the natural senses and believe God's Word using His faith. If you consider God's Word to be true, then you cannot accept your natural senses as evidence since they depend on your physical self and the tangible and visible world. Faith, on the other hand, belongs to your spiritual self; it brings the invisible into existence and makes that which is in eternity manifest in the natural world. In other words, it makes the invisible visible; the impossible, possible, the intangible, tangible.

> Having faith in God's Word is
> always pleasing to God.

Testimony: A gentleman had spent eight months—24 hours a day—connected to an oxygen machine due to an illness called, Pulmonary Fibrosis, which causes scarring of the lungs, making it difficult to breath. He was invited to come to the church by someone he did not know. That same day, he went up to the altar and by faith he removed the oxygen mask. He received God's faith, believed as God believes, and was healed instantly.

Faith and Reason

Anyone might get the wrong idea and believe that faith is blind, but when reason argues with it, faith laughs in its face. Faith moves and operates the same way God does. While reason worries and gets nervous, faith is firm and unshakeable; the person of faith knows that God cannot lie because His divine nature does not allow it. God gave us faith the moment we received Jesus as our Lord and Savior; that is when we also received eternal life—the same life that God has, full of His faith. Hence, Jesus tells you today: "Have the faith of God."

> Faith knows and believes what
> reason has yet to discover.

Review

■ Living by faith means to live life to the fullest; to rejoice, flourish, to recover our health, live uninterruptedly, to be saved, and much more.

- Anything we do without faith is a sin and is void of God's life.

- We can live by sight or by faith; the choice is ours.

- To live by sight is to depend on our natural senses and knowledge; to live by faith is God's will for us.

- Faith is not a magic thing, an emergency kit, knowledge, hope, or presumption.

- Faith is for now; hope is for the future. Hope is a step before faith, but it cannot take anything from eternity.

- Faith is the substance, the title deed of what we hope for; the certainty that the miracle is ours, ready for the taking.

- Faith is conviction, the irrefutable proof or the firm testimony that what we believe has already taken place in the spirit realm and therefore can be manifested in the natural realm.

- Faith believes what God believes.

- Faith cannot create; it can only obtain what God created with His words.

- There are over 30,000 promises in the Bible; these form part of our God-given inheritance.

- Everyone receives a measure of faith. As we exercise it, God will give us more.

- The two sources from which we receive and develop our faith are: God's Word and Rhema. Both are given by God and impressed in our spirit, and they never contradict each other.

171

- Faith is loosened by our confession. If we confess the same that God spoke in the eternal realm, there is nothing that can stand in the way of making that confession materialize in the natural.

- For faith to be effective it must be confessed and a corresponding action must be taken.

- The prayer of faith loosens God's power, but it does not always mean our prayer will manifest immediately.

- Symptoms are completely irrelevant to faith. Faith goes above and beyond the symptoms. If these persist after believing, the declaration of faith will cause them to stop.

- Reason cannot argue or compete with faith because both belong to different dimensions; they are incompatible. Faith knows and believes what reason has yet to discover.

Final Prayers

Dear friend, if you are in need of a miracle, if you are experiencing a crisis, or if you are sick and no one has ever taught you the things I have covered in this chapter, then let me ask you, "Would you like to receive God's faith through His Son? Jesus has eternal life to give you; the same type of life God has. If you want God's faith and eternal life, please pray the following prayer out loud. Otherwise, let me remind you that without His faith, you will not be able to believe like He does regardless of how much personal effort you put into it. The Lord must give you of His faith for you to receive, for you to be able to please Him, and for you to be able to impart unto others the same blessings you have received today." Repeat after me, out loud:

Heavenly Father, in the name of Jesus, I recognize that I am a sinner. I repent of all my sins and confess that Jesus is the Son of God. I believe, with all my heart, that You raised Him from the dead. Today I receive Your faith because Jesus now lives in my heart. He has given me eternal life, and my healing is in His life.

Now allow me to pray for you. It is my heart's desire for you to receive your physical, material, or emotional miracle or for God to supply any need you might have.

Heavenly Father, I pray for every person reading this book who is sick and in need of a miracle. I rebuke the spirit of infirmity and order it to leave their bodies right now. Lord, by faith, they extend their hands into eternity and receive their healing. By faith they confess it and receive it right now. I declare them healed!

If you confessed these prayers, begin to do what you were unable to do before. Declare it out loud: "In the name of Jesus, I am healed. I am free!" If you were physically ill, I rebuke every oppressing spirit and declare that they leave right now. Begin to move and to do what you couldn't do. Begin to take the corresponding action because faith without works is dead. You gain nothing by confessing without taking action. Turn your confession into the corresponding action. If you are bound to a wheelchair, stand up. If you couldn't move your arm, move it. If you had difficulty breathing, take deep breaths. If you couldn't run, run now. If you had palpable cysts or tumors, check yourself. Take the corresponding action! If you believe for a business, begin to make the necessary legal transactions to make it happen. If you don't know which corresponding action to make, ask the Holy Spirit to guide you, and you will have the victory. I pray this chapter has blessed your life. Keep in mind that the righteous live by faith and this is necessary to receive God's blessings, to please Him, and to bless others.

Note:

To pray with Apostle Guillermo Maldonado and receive his powerful impartation, visit: kingjesus.org/jesus-heals-prayer

CHAPTER VIII

STEPS TO RECEIVING YOUR HEALING

*L*et us take a moment to put everything into perspective. Picture Jesus and His newly recruited disciples and answer some common questions. What Bible did they use? They used the Old Testament Scrolls because the New Testament had not been written yet. This being so, what did they testify about? They would preach of God and His powerful deeds. Jesus would visually reveal the Kingdom of God because they were unable to conceptualize its greatness. He helped His disciples abandon their religiosity and legalistic points of view. More importantly, He also taught them to know God as their Father and thus establish a close and intimate relationship with Him. The Old Testament is history; nonetheless it references events that would take place in the future, thousands of years later. Among its many books, the book of Isaiah is rich in prophecies that were fulfilled by our Savior, Jesus; specifically, these can be found in chapters 40-66 and are also known as the "Old Testament Gospel."

Isaiah makes special emphasis on not living in sin and thus compromising our principles. He states that if Jesus died for us, we should no longer have to live in sin but under the grace of everything that Jesus did for us on the Cross. The prophet perceived this to be a divine exchange in which every physical, spiritual, and emotional need was provided for us through Jesus' perfect sacrifice. Therefore, everything we might do to dampen the event of the Cross will lead to falsifying the truth. The Cross is, without question, the center of the Gospel's provision.

Surely He has borne our griefs and carried our sorrows; yet we esteemed Him stricken, smitten by God, and afflicted.

But He was wounded for our transgressions, He was bruised for our iniquities; the chastisement for our peace was upon Him, and by His stripes we are healed. All we like sheep have gone astray; We have turned, every one, to his own way; and the LORD has laid on Him the iniquity of us all.
ISAIAH 53:4-6

This verse is right at the center of the 66 chapters of Isaiah. The main problem of mankind is that they lose God's way by choosing their own path. God calls this iniquity. Avon is the word for *iniquity* in the Hebrew language, and it also means rebellion. This is the very essence of selfishness that motivates us to do our own will. This is a universal evil found in every race, ethnic background, and nations of the world. Everyone is a rebel by inheritance of Adam's sin. Yet, we are able to receive God's love and forgiveness because the Father placed humanity's collective iniquity upon Jesus' body and nailed it on the Cross. As I said before, a divine exchange took place at the Cross of Calvary: It was there that the punishment we deserved was placed upon Jesus—He gave Himself in exchange for the forgiveness of our sins. This occurred by none other than the fact that God decided it to be so. This is the essence of God's grace: For Him to freely give us something that we have done nothing to deserve. There is no way we could have ever earned or deserved what Jesus did at the Cross. The only way to receive this gift is by believing. Therefore, let us stop trying to earn our inheritance from Jesus because we cannot pay for it (for it has been paid for), we can only embrace it.

What is Jesus called?

And so it is written, 'The first man Adam became a living being.' The last Adam became a life-giving spirit.

However, the spiritual is not first, but the natural, and afterward the spiritual. The first man was of the earth, made of dust; the second Man is the Lord from heaven. **1 CORINTHIANS 15:45-47**

These verses call Jesus the last Adam and the Second Man. He was the **last Adam** at the Cross because that is where the wickedness of mankind was placed, originating in the first human being from the onset of creation to this day and into the future. All the sin and wickedness of mankind was placed upon Jesus, and when He was raised from the dead, He did it as the **Second Man**—Emmanuel, God among us. He was the first to establish a new race, a new generation (Vincent, 2009).

What specifically took place during the divine exchange of the Cross?

■ **Jesus suffered the punishment so that we could receive His peace**

Jesus took upon Himself that punishment for our sin so that we could be forgiven, resulting in peace. God says that the wages of sin is death, and since He does not compromise His principles, He took it upon Himself to deal with our sins before He could freely give is His peace. This is the reason the old man (old nature) has to die, crucified, together with Christ. When sin dies, Jesus, who is pure and holy, rises up within us as in the resurrection; when this occurs, we obtain peace with God, with ourselves, and with others.

Therefore, having been justified by faith, we have peace with God through our Lord Jesus Christ. **ROMANS 5:1**

> The essence of Jesus' sacrifice was the exchange
> that took place, which as God Himself
> ordained, would provide everything mankind
> could ever need, both in the spiritual realm
> (eternity) and the physical realm (time).

When we receive forgiveness of our sin, we receive redemption; this means to repurchase or reacquire what we originally owned. Let us look at it this way: Mankind belonged to God until sin came and we became Satan's property. However, at the Cross, we were given back to God because Jesus shed His blood to pay the price of our rescue.

■ **He took upon His body our pain and sickness so that we could live in health**

The physical aspect of the Cross is that Jesus took our sickness and pain; thus, providing healing to our bodies. Interestingly enough, when the Word mentions the Cross, it never places healing as a future event, rather it is always written in past tense; in other words, as Jesus said, *"It is finished!"* (John 19:30). This means that we were healed from the foundation of the world when Jesus died for us.

How do I know if it is God's will to heal me?

The question a new believer asks should not be *if* it is God's will to heal him, but how they can receive the healing that Jesus already provided for him. If people fail to believe that God already provided their healing, how can they grab hold of it? It is fundamental to recognize that God did provide for our healing at the Cross. In Jesus' ministry, there is no distinction between healing and casting out demons; both signs go hand in hand.

When evening had come, they brought to Him many who were demon-possessed. And He cast out the spirits with a word, and healed all who were sick. **MATTHEW 8:16**

Jesus taught, preached, healed, and casted out demons. Why?

That it might be fulfilled which was spoken by Isaiah the prophet, saying: 'He Himself took our infirmities and bore our sicknesses.' **MATTHEW 8:17**

This verse demonstrates that healing and salvation go hand in hand. The evidence that He took our sickness is that He healed all that went to Him who were sick. The Bible always emphasizes the pronoun "Him" to avoid any misunderstandings of God's identity. Peter also talks in this same direction:

...Who Himself bore our sins in His own body on the tree, that we, having died to sins, might live for righteousness—by whose stripes you were healed. **1 PETER 2:24**

Once again, we see that God is referred to as "Himself."

When Jesus declared that it was done—perfected, completed, finished, and that there was nothing left to be done because it was all paid for at the Cross—He was talking about salvation. Interestingly enough, the word *salvation* found in the New Testament is the translation from the Greek word *sozo* which means healing! *Soteria* is also used which means *salvation*. The point is that the words used for salvation derive from words that also mean *healing*.

Testimony: Once I met a young man who was visiting our church for the first time. His legs had been crushed in a car accident. Even after many operations, he had to use a cane to help him walk. Andres had forgotten what it felt like to walk effortlessly, much less run or jump. However, the day he accepted the Lord, he decided to take hold of the entire package of salvation. In the beginning, his corresponding action was to stop using the cane. Then he tried running on the altar. He succeeded and enjoyed this wonderful experience once again! This is where the package of salvation was manifested in its entirety.

Let's look at a Biblical example of what we are talking about.

The Woman with the Issue of Blood

> For she said within herself, If I may but touch his garment, I shall be whole. But Jesus turned him about, and when he saw her, he said, Daughter, be of good comfort; thy faith hath made thee whole. And the woman was made whole from that hour. **MATTHEW 9:21, 22—KJV**

In the days of Jesus, when a woman on her period would touch a man, he would be immediately considered impure. Therefore, when the woman with the issue of blood touched Jesus, she actually broke the law. However, instead of feeling impure or rebuking her, He said to her, *"Thy faith hath made thee whole."* When Jesus said she was whole, it meant that she was healed, saved, and delivered. There are many other instances similar to this one in which salvation, deliverance, and even the resurrection of the dead takes place in relation to healing. In other words, the salvation Jesus provided us at the Cross includes all the above; it is a complete package.

How do we take hold of the healing that Jesus provided for us at the Cross?

1. Faith

...Without faith it is impossible to please Him, for he who comes to God must believe that He is, and that He is a rewarder of those who diligently seek Him. **HEBREWS 11:6**

Faith is an essential element required in order to receive your healing. It is interesting to note two very important things mentioned in this verse: It is not enough to know that He exists, but we must also be fully aware that if we seek Him, wholeheartedly, we will be rewarded. Faith is essential, but diligence—the action of seeking Him—is also vital. The Bible teaches that laziness is the opposite of diligence, saying that laziness is a sin. It also points out the countless blessings that await those who are diligent. The Word also condemns laziness more than drunkenness. Sadly, many people in the church today are lazy. We should know that God does not reward laziness; hence, we must place our priorities in order and work. Furthermore, we must believe that God will reward our diligence with healing if we choose to seek Him and only Him.

What is the source of our faith?

So then faith comes by hearing, and hearing by the word of God. **ROMANS 10:17**

People tend to interpret this verse as *faith comes by hearing God's Word;* but, what the Bible really says is that the ability to hear God comes from the Word, and the ability to have faith comes from hearing. There are two stages in which this takes place:

- **Hearing God's Word, continuously**

When you hear God's Word with all your heart and mind, the first thing you receive is the ability to hear by faith. The problem most people have is that they give little time to hearing and even less time to allow what they hear to produce faith. For this reason, it is necessary to expose yourself to His Word without limitations of time. Hearing does not necessarily come from reading the Bible. Please don't misunderstand me. You must read it, but beyond that, you must read it continuously—as stated in the verse—so that as you hear the Word it produces faith in your heart. For example: I listen continuously to hundreds of teachings and messages of godly men and women which I have stored in my IPod. Whether traveling, at home, or when I retire for the night, I listen to them because I understand this principle: faith does not come just by hearing the Word; it comes by hearing it continuously.

- **Hearing comes through a Rhema word given specifically by God**

But He answered and said, 'It is written, 'Man shall not live by bread alone, but by every word that proceeds from the mouth of God.' **MATTHEW 4:4**

We live by God's Rhema—the word He continuously and presently speaks into our spirits, thus becoming real

184

to those who perceive it. That is the bread Jesus said we should be eating for life. In the original scrolls, the word proceed indicates a continuous and permanent action. Realistically speaking, the Bible is simply a "black book with white pages filled with black and red letters", which in and of itself, cannot produce anything except give knowledge, like many books do. What makes it different and gives it the power to transform mere words into faith is the Holy Spirit. He breathes life into each word. This is the reason many can read the Bible from start to finish and remain atheists; they study it as a mere work of literature, choosing not to believe is inspired by God.

> The Holy Spirit vivifies God's Word in us.

Faith comes by hearing. Each time we hear, our faith grows as the Holy Spirit breathes life into each word. Instant faith is non-existent to God, but we are so used to having everything the moment we ask for it that when God doesn't produce what we want (as if He were a microwave or a money-making machine) we get discouraged.

Testimony: A lady who was born with one leg shorter than the other visited our church. This problem had caused her to suffer with scoliosis, producing the muscles in her back to stiffen due to her bad posture and the awkward way she had to walk. The pain she suffered was intense, but in one crusade, she heard the Word and the Holy Spirit made it take life in her. The power of God came upon her body and she was completely healed. She later attended one of our regular services because she also had arthritis in one foot in addition to allergies. By the power of the Holy Spirit, she received healing for this as well.

How do we receive the Word?

For this reason we also thank God without ceasing, because when you received the word of God which you heard from us, you welcomed it not as the word of men, but as it is in truth, the word of God, which also effectively works in you who believe. **1 THESSALONIANS 2:13**

• As God's Word

Respect the Bible for what it is: God's Word and not man's word. We must accept that God will do everything He promised to do.

• With humility

But be doers of the word, and not hearers only, deceiving yourselves. **JAMES 1:22**

We must receive the Word with humility. Recognizing that God is the Teacher and we are His disciples; thus, as His students, we cannot tell the Teacher what to do or when to do it. Remember, faith requires us to take God's Word seriously when we read it. And to read it with faith is to appropriate God's promises; to believe what we are reading with certainty that He will keep His word. Therefore, when God asks us to take a specific action, we should quickly obey.

> The best time to persist with faith is when you seek God but nothing seems to take place.

186

2. The Holy Spirit is the administrator of our salvation

Another way to take possession of our healing is through the Holy Spirit. He is the only administrator of our salvation; the only one capable of opening the treasures of God's grace, mysteries, provision, and abundance. Yet, He continues to be seriously ignored in the Church. Much is said of Him but He is still ignored. If we want healing and every blessing God has provided, we must befriend the Holy Spirit—He is a person and the third person of the Deity: Father, Son, and Holy Spirit. One of the most powerful experiences in the life of a Christian is to learn to have an intimate relationship with the Holy Spirit. We must invite Him to our services and allow Him the right to move as He wills. He is the only person in the universe who does not seek attention to Himself. Perhaps this is the reason we fail to acknowledge Him.

He will glorify Me, for He will take of what is Mine and declare it to you. **JOHN 16:14**

The best way to prove that something comes from God is if you can answer Yes to the following question: Does this glorify Jesus Christ? If we are glorifying an individual, a doctrine, or a denomination, then it does not come from God because the Holy Spirit does not glorify such things. Rather, if we want to draw the Holy Spirit closer we need to be glorifying Christ. Thus, when we raise our hands in praise and worship Jesus, the Holy Spirit makes Himself present in our church services and guides us into receiving what God has for us.

All things that the Father has are Mine. Therefore I said that He will take of Mine and declare it to you. **JOHN 16:15**

Here Jesus confirms that the Holy Spirit is the only one who has the key to God's treasures. Everything the Father and Son have is managed by the Holy Spirit; therefore, it is worth becoming His friend.

Why should we be guided by the Holy Spirit?

For as many as are led by the Spirit of God, these are sons of God. ROMANS 8:14

The word led, in this verse, means: to guide, lead, direct; to show the way. This implies maturity because if we are led by the Spirit of God, then we are not merely governed by rules, procedures, methods, councils, technicalities, or others (although these are good, they cannot always be trusted); rather, we are trusting, relying on, and allowing ourselves to be guided by the Holy Spirit, who is sure to always give us the victory.

Modern psychology has its rules, principles, and statistics used to diagnose people according to its own parameters; but, this is not necessarily the best way of diagnosing people's illnesses. We do not need to accept their results because we are to trust in the Holy Spirit above all else. If anyone tries to make sense of you through a series of questionnaires, don't trust in the results; these are simple tools that may be able to help you, but these should never supersede our trust in God—our full trust should be in Him, alone. When you learn to totally depend on the Holy Spirit, He will take of what Jesus has and give it to you—in this case, your healing.

3. Believe wholeheartedly

For with the heart one believes unto righteousness, and with the mouth confession is made unto salvation. ROMANS 10:10

Another way to appropriate your healing is by believing, wholeheartedly. Many say they believe but what they are really doing is exercising mental faith. This type of faith begins as head-knowledge, but it never becomes heartfelt conviction; hence, many fail to get their healing. What does it mean to believe? In the Greek language, the word pisteuo is translated as believe which means: to be persuaded; to place confidence in, to surrender, or to attach oneself to something or someone until results are obtained. If we take these definitions, we can say that belief is one's ability to be persuaded by God in knowing that His Word is true.

Who shall witness signs and wonders?

And these signs will follow those who believe: In My name they will cast out demons; they will speak with new tongues.
MARK 16:17

These signs and wonders will follow those who believe. In other words, if you believe you shall see; if you don't believe, the signs will not follow you. If you are sick and believe, these signs will follow you. In addition, you will also be able to impart that healing unto others when you pray and lay hands on them, in the name of Jesus.

4. Your confession

But what does it say? 'The word is near you, in your mouth and in your heart' (that is, the word of faith which we preach): 9that if you confess with your mouth the Lord Jesus and believe in your heart that God has raised Him from the dead, you will be saved. 10For with the heart one believes

189

unto righteousness and with the mouth confession is made unto salvation. **ROMANS 10:8-10**

There is something interesting in these verses. In verses eight and nine, the Apostle Paul mentions the mouth before the heart; but in verse ten, the heart is mentioned first. The proper use of your mouth and the proper answer of your heart will make the word of faith manifest because the mouth serves as a channel to faith.

In Western society, we tend to say that we learn or know something "by heart," but in Hebrew the expression declares that we learn "by mouth."—It is a Hebrew tradition to repeat something, over and over again, until it is settled and imbedded in their hearts.

...That if you confess with your mouth the Lord Jesus and believe in your heart that God has raised Him from the dead, you will be saved. **ROMANS 10:9**

In this verse, the mouth is mentioned before the heart:

For with the heart one believes unto righteousness and with the mouth confession is made unto salvation. **ROMANS 10:10**

In this verse, the heart is mentioned before the mouth.

What is confession?

The word confession is the translation for the Greek word *homologeo*, which means: to make the same declaration; in this case, it means to stand in agreement with God in regard to your testimony. Thus, confess or make the same declarations that He makes in His Word concerning sin, sickness, failures, health, victory, and anything else in your life. In other words, recognize, confirm, and ratify what God has already said. For example, if you are sick and experiencing the symptoms of the disease, what should you be declaring? You cannot declare or confess the symptoms; instead, you must establish God's Word—resist the enemy and the deceiving symptoms he sends to your body and confess God's Word: "By His stripes I was healed."

By confessing His Word and promises you are claiming your legal rights before God's throne. A synonym of the word, confession, is the word professing which means: to say and accept what one believes; therefore, we are to say what God says and be in agreement with Him, recognizing His Word as the only truth.

Therefore, holy brethren, partakers of the heavenly calling, consider the Apostle and High Priest of our confession, Christ Jesus. **HEBREWS 3:1**

Jesus is our High Priest; the one who presents our confession before the Father. If we don't confess His Word, then Jesus doesn't have anything to confess to the Father about us.

> To confess is to affirm what we believe; to testify what we know; to endorse or validate the truth. God's Word is the exclusive object of our confession and testimony.

You need to learn to stand firm against anything that contradicts God's Word—natural senses, symptoms, and

191

thoughts sent by the enemy—and believe and declare it to be true. For example: if you have the physical evidence proving that you have an incurable disease, then you need to boldly declare that Jesus took your sickness, your illness, your disease on the Cross, and that Satan has no legal right to impose any of them on your body. You must affirm, believing it, that by His stripes you were healed. Confess it out loud. Confront the physical evidence with your confession and make a commitment that you will testify to others that God healed you. Doing so will help you stand firm and declare Jesus' testimony.

The wrong confession leads to defeat and failure, and it implicitly declares the enemy's supremacy; therefore, decide to speak as God speaks because that confession will make your faith grow and eventually defeat the adversary, every time.

Testimony: A gentleman suffered serious head trauma, forcing the doctors to intubate him. After 12 days in the hospital, his wife was told that he had less than three days to live. At the news, she went before God's presence in prayer. With the help of another lady in church, they both stood in agreement and began to declare His Word, speaking healing and deliverance over her husband's life. Little by little, he began to recover. A few weeks later, he left the hospital totally healed. Praise God, for their combined confession of God's Word produced a miracle when there seemed to be no hope.

...Who Himself bore our sins in His own body on the tree, that we, having died to sins, might live for righteousness—by whose stripes you were healed. **1 PETER 2:24**

How do you confess the Word?

It is very easy to confess God's Word; all you have to do is simply repeat the following: "Jesus bore my sickness and illness at the Cross." After confessing the Word, it is quite possible for the pain or symptom to still remain, but don't give up. Continue confessing it. "I stand firm on my confession, regardless of what I feel. By His stripes I was healed." It is important to keep your confession until the healing becomes evident. Remember that doing this is not a matter of mindlessly and mechanically repeating words by memory, for that is vain repetition. Rather, you need to declare the Word with faith, holding fast to the healing power of God's Word, and then watch the miracles come to life.

5. To receive your healing, you must act in faith

What does it profit, my brethren, if someone says he has faith but does not have works? Can faith save him?
JAMES 2:14

It is worthless to say that you believe in anything if you fail to accompany it with a corresponding action. If you claim to be healed then you should act accordingly; stop telling people you are healed one moment and sick the next. Keep your confession consistent in word and action. Who can guide you on what action(s) to take? The Holy Spirit can. He will show you what corresponding action to take according to your faith. Allow Him to lead you.

I know of a man who was healed by God but was afraid to testify the miracle. Consequently, he fell ill again and lived in that devastated state for a long time, until he asked God to forgive him and was healed once more.

Thereafter, he continually testified of what God had done for his body and heart.

After believing and confessing the right words, there is one more thing you must do: take the appropriate action, because faith without action is dead. God's Word is medicine to our bodies and the Holy Spirit will always guide us to take the right corresponding action. He will never ask you to do the same thing, but He will inspire you to act. Some might faithfully declare that God will heal them, and so they choose not to take their medication; this could be the right course of action to take or not—the Holy Spirit will let them know. I have never asked anyone to stop their medical treatment or to stop taking their medication because I understand that God uses doctors as channels of blessings to heal people. If it were not for them, many would die before their time. However, there are people who refuse to be seen by a doctor, not because of their faith but because they are afraid of the diagnosis.

You must always be very attentive to the Holy Spirit's voice and guidance; this is simply an act of faith. Therefore, discover what He wants you to do and do it! If the Holy Spirit guides you to stop taking your medicine or to stop going to the doctor, that is a personal and private decision between the two of you. However, I can assure you that if God guides you to do it, it is because you are healed. Amen.

Testimony: While ministering in a men's conference, God revealed to me that one of them had diabetes. The man was losing his eyesight due to this vile disease, but when I prayed for him, the Holy Spirit convicted him of his healing. He took the medication he had been taking for years and threw them on the floor, stomping on them. Weeks later, he went to the doctor who discovered that his sugar level was normal, and the diabetes had disappeared. My advice to you is to never make the corresponding action without the leading of the Holy Spirit. Only He can guide you to do it and show you how to go about it; as it happened with this man.

6. You will receive healing through thanksgiving

In everything give thanks; for this is the will of God in Christ Jesus for you. **1 THESSALONIANS 5:18**

Many people find themselves outside of God's will because they fail to be grateful.

> The simplest act of faith is to give thanks; this is something anyone can do.

Jesus was Grateful

...Jesus took the loaves, and when He had given thanks He distributed them to the disciples, and the disciples to those sitting down; and likewise of the fish, as much as they wanted. **JOHN 6:11**

Jesus didn't make a sophisticated prayer. He simply said, "Thank you!" His gratitude loosened the power to multiply the bread and fish. The Apostle John was so impressed by this that he, too, learned to give thanks.

Testimony: I met a woman addicted to cocaine, alcohol, and other drugs for three years. When I spoke with her, she confessed that her son attended our church and was interceding for her to be free of these addictions. Every day he would declare God's Word and give thanks for the miracle. When she finally visited the church, the Lord immediately delivered her. This miracle took place because a young man decided to stand in the gap for his mother, with thankfulness, because his faith gave him the conviction that the miracle was already done.

Review

The steps to receiving your healing are: faith, seeking God diligently until you see the manifestation of what you are waiting for, hearing His Word continuously, believing wholeheartedly, confessing God's Word/promise, and taking the corresponding action to your faith as led by the Holy Spirit.

- Jesus was the Last Adam and the Second Man. When He was raised from the dead, He left the first Adam and every one of his sins behind in the tomb.

- The two characteristics of the divine exchange that took place at the Cross are: Jesus suffered the punishment, so we could receive His peace (reconciliation with God), and Jesus bore our sickness and pain so we could receive His healing.

- Salvation includes bodily healing and deliverance.

- To take ownership of your healing, Jesus provided six steps which we are to follow:

  - Faith is essential to receiving healing. Without it, God's power cannot be activated to produce the miracle; to develop it you must hear His written Word and the

Rhema word continuously. The Holy Spirit will vivify His Word in us if we receive it with a humble heart and with conviction that it comes from Him.

- Recognize that the Holy Spirit is the administrator of your salvation. This means that you should establish a close and intimate relationship with Him, for He is the only One who can give you access to His countless treasures.

- Believe and allow yourself to be persuaded by God. Trust and lean on Him and surrender to His promises.

- Confess the Word by speaking what God speaks; this increases your faith because you are aligning your words to the Holy Spirit's guidance.

- Act by faith; this is the direct result of hearing and confessing God's Word continuously. Taking the corresponding action puts your miracle in motion.

- Always be grateful. You should always be grateful and thankful for your healing, miracle, and deliverance.

Final Prayer

At this time, I want to pray for everyone who is sick. If you need a healing miracle or any other type of miracle, I want to pray for you. Now you understand that faith is founded on the fact that Jesus died on the Cross; that He bore our sickness and pain, so we could be healed. If you did not receive healing as you read this book, this is the moment of truth. Allow me to pray, while you receive it in faith:

Heavenly Father, at this time, I thank you for every reader of this book. I ask that you open their eyes and unveil Your truth before them, so they can clearly see Jesus' wonderful and redeeming work. He took your place and mine so that we could be healed of any sickness and forgiven of all our sins. Right now, I exercise authority over every spirit of infirmity in your body and order them to leave. Every spirit of death and sickness has to go now from your bodies. I declare you healed and delivered, in the name of Jesus, Amen!

Now I ask you to begin declaring the following, out loud: *"By His stripes I was healed. I am healed. I believe that God's Word is truth and I take hold of the complete, redeeming work at the Cross. I thank You, Lord, because I am healed. I speak Your Word against every symptom and thought sent by the enemy, and I declare total healing in my body; in the name of Jesus, Amen!"*

Dear reader, I ask you now to take a corresponding action by faith. Please begin to do something that the sickness kept you from doing. If you could not move your foot, begin to move it. Stop seeking the illness and begin looking for your healing. Take the step of faith. If your previous condition prevented you from verifying your healing, then simply raise your hands before the Lord and begin to praise Him and give Him thanks for your healing. You are healed and delivered because Jesus paid the full price at the Cross of Calvary.

Note:

To pray with Apostle Guillermo Maldonado and receive his powerful impartation, visit: kingjesus.org/jesus-heals-prayer

CHAPTER IX

HOW TO KEEP YOUR HEALING

*T*he last thing we expect to see after someone is healed by God's power is to see them suffering again with the same illness. When this happens, it seems contrary to His Word, and we begin to wonder, "Could it be that the person failed to pray as he should have?" Is it possible that God took back his healing? Could it be a curse? What could cause someone to lose their healing, get even worse than before, and die?

Over the years I have discovered a sad truth: among the people God heals, some lose their healing after a certain period of time. The reason for this occurrence varies. I must admit this was hard for me to understand. Sadly, the same happens with deliverance. I have ministered deliverance to many who were delivered of demonic influences, only to discover that, after some time, they were experiencing the same oppression or worse. Hence, in this chapter, I will use God's Word and my experience to explain why people lose their healing.

Reasons one can lose their healing:

1. **One's healing can be lost when it is received through someone else's faith.**

   Let us observe two completely different instances found in the Bible. First, the widow from Nain mentioned in Luke 7:11 whose son was raised from the dead by Jesus' faith and compassion—not her own. The widow represents the type of person who receives her petition by way of a miracle, yet is unable to be a channel of blessings to others because she received her miracle through someone else's faith; in this case, it was by Jesus' faith. Knowing this, we can conclude that many of those who fail to retain their miracle lose it because they lack foundation and knowledge in the Word. Therefore, when the enemy attacks them with symptoms or thoughts designed to steal their healing, they are unable to resist and become ill again.

On the other hand, there are people who have developed their faith, and like the woman from Canaan (Matthew 15), hear the Word and believe it. Specifically, the woman of Canaan underwent a process and developed her faith greatly with the help of Jesus. After receiving her daughter's miraculous healing, she was also blessed with a complete training on the Word; hence, she was able to stand firm on the Word of God and continue being a channel of blessings and healing for others. The point I am trying to make is that both cases establish a very clear principle: If someone lacks the biblical foundation on healing and is healed by another's faith instead of their own, they may not be able to resist the enemy's attacks and risk losing their healing.

2. Healing can be lost when the enemy is given a foothold

...nor give place to the devil. EPHESIANS 4:27

There are many venues that can give the devil a foothold, granting him access to our lives and exposing us to his attacks; for example, envy, unforgiveness, judgment, disagreements, bitterness, anger, and much more. These are invitations that open the door for the enemy to come in; therefore, we must close every door to the enemy and prevent him from attacking our bodies with sickness over and over again. We must understand that the enemy does not have any authority over us; rather, we have the power to rebuke and expel him, regardless of the symptoms or thoughts he sends our way. So, let us shut the door and get rid of him, we have the authority to do it!

Testimony: I once prayed for a woman who had been diagnosed with cancer. When she returned to her doctor, she was given a clean bill of health; she brought in her results as a testimony of her healing. A year later, I was informed that the cancer had returned, stronger than before, and died a short time later. At this my wife and I had to ask the Lord what had happened because we were having a hard time understanding. We both felt there had been unforgiveness in her heart against her ex-husband. Sometime later, after having a few conversations with people who were close to her we confirmed that she did, in fact, hold unforgiveness in her heart. This gave the devil a foothold into her life, causing the cancer to return and take her life. Now do you realize the importance of refusing to give the enemy a foothold?

3. Faith based on physical evidence rather than on God's Word

Another reason why people lose their healing is faith based on physical evidence. When people hear that someone was healed or see it firsthand, hope and faith rise to believe for their own miracle. They receive their healing instantly, but when the enemy comes to steal it away, they are unable to defend it because their faith is not based on God's Word. They can repeat the phrase, over and over again, "By His stripes I am healed," but if they lack the conviction that this gift belongs to them, and believe only on physical evidence, they will be unable to fight off the enemy when he comes to take their healing miracle away; therefore, the sickness returns.

4. A negative confession

Death and life are in the power of the tongue, and those who love it will eat its fruit. **PROVERBS 18:21**

Many people pretend to be healthy but continually contemplate death, constantly complaining of bodily aches. We cannot believe one thing and confess the opposite. When we open our mouths and speak sickness and disease, we open the door to the spirit of sickness to enter our bodies; as a result, we begin/continue experiencing the symptoms. Thus, it is imperative that we speak God's Word and cast out every spirit of sickness and death.

5. A lifestyle of sin

Afterward Jesus found him in the temple, and said to him, 'See, you have been made well. Sin no more, lest a worse thing come upon you.' **JOHN 5:14**

Another reason why people lose their healing is because they continue to willingly live in sin. Jesus said, "Go and sin no more!" In other words, "You are healed! Now go and stop sinning; otherwise, something worse is going to come upon you." In essence, Jesus was saying that if we continue living a lifestyle of sin, our actions will give the enemy the legal right to enter our lives and do what he wants, in this case, make us sick again.

Testimony: A body builder came to our church, received the Lord, and was saved. Shortly after, he was diagnosed with terminal cancer. He came to the altar during one of our services and we prayed for him. God healed him! Afterwards, he went to the doctor who diagnosed that he was totally healed. This man continued to attend our church, but a year later his heart started to grow cold, barely coming to any worship services. After a year, he returned; it was then that I noticed his weak and sickly physical state. I asked him what was wrong and he said that the cancer had returned. I reminded him that God had already healed him; he had the papers to prove it. He then replied that he didn't know why the cancer had returned. At that moment, his son who was nearby spoke up saying, "Daddy, you can't lie to the pastor. Tell him what you have been doing." Instantly he admitted that he had been fornicating (living with a woman outside the marriage relationship) and he believed that was the reason the cancer had returned. He opened the door to that sickness when he returned to sin. This time, the cancer came back full force and killed him. This should serve as a warning to all of us. If God heals us, we cannot continue to live in sin. We must confess our sin, repent, and separate from it; this is the only way to prevent any sickness from touching our bodies.

6. It is a mystery

Sometimes it is a mystery why people lose their healing. I have known people who were not living in sin and had no open doors to the enemy; they would confess life continually and lived correctly before God, and still they lost their healing. Why? I don't have the answer; we will probably understand this when we get to Heaven. For now, the most important thing for us to do is not focus on why people lose their healing, because for everyone person who loses his/her healing, there are hundreds that keep it.

I know many people who were healed of cancer and are still enjoying full health today. Others have been healed of AIDS and continue to be in good health. More people retain their healing and deliverance than those who lose it; one case of someone losing it should not derail us. We can't be questioning God all the time as to why this happens. We should just believe His Word, confess it, and close every door to the enemy; thus, avoiding a worse fate.

Steps to Keeping your Healing

1. Make Jesus the absolute Lord in every area of your life

You make Jesus the absolute Lord in every area of your life by freely choosing to do so and through confession. For example, you can say, "Jesus, you are the Lord of my life, my emotions, my attitudes, my mind, my sexual life, my money, my family, and my church; in fact, everything belongs to you! I now choose, of my own free will, to make you Lord of every area of my life. I submit to your Lordship." Doing this is like taking the keys to every room in your home and handing them over to a trustworthy person.

Why should this be done?

When an unclean spirit goes out of a man, he goes through dry places, seeking rest, and finds none. Then he says, 'I will return to my house from which I came.' And when he comes, he finds it empty, swept, and put in order. Then he goes and takes with him seven other spirits more wicked than himself, and they enter and dwell there; and the last state of that man is worse than the first. So shall it also be with this wicked generation. **MATTHEW 12:43-45**

When do you expose yourself to the enemy's attacks? You expose yourself when you leave your house unattended and empty. In other words, when a spirit of sickness is cast out, it leaves a void that must be filled with Jesus; this is the reason Jesus must be Lord of every area in your life.

Illustration: When you take a road trip and reach nightfall, you begin to look for a place to spend the night, and so you become very attentive to places that have a vacant sign. When you see the neon sign, you stop and enter. Spirits of infirmity, sickness, and disease do the same; when they are cast out, they begin to seek a place to rest. If they can't find one, they will return to the place where they left; hence, the importance to fill the void they leave behind with Jesus.

> Every area occupied by Jesus is secure, but the areas where Jesus is not Lord are vulnerable.

If Jesus has healed or delivered you and you are still refusing to totally surrender to His Lordship, you have a neon sign in the spirit realm that says "vacant." It will not take long before a wicked spirit comes into your life to oppress, torment, and make you sick. Remember two things: the devil's agenda is to kill, steal, and destroy, and you are not strong enough to keep him out of your house on own your own—but Jesus is. When Jesus is the Lord of your life, in charge of every area, no demon is strong enough to oppress you. You will be kept safe!

2. Be continually full of the Holy Spirit.

Once you are filled with the Holy Spirit, with the evidence of speaking in other tongues, the Word of God teaches that you need to be continually full of His Spirit.

On the last day, that great day of the feast, Jesus stood and cried out, saying, 'If anyone thirsts, let him come to Me and drink.' **JOHN 7:37**

This verse is written in the present perfect tense. With this in mind, this verse actually says, "Come and continue coming; drink and continue drinking of the river of the Holy Spirit." Drinking of God's water—or being filled with God's Holy Spirit—is not something we are meant to experience just once, when get saved; rather, we are to continuously choose to be filled and surrender every area of our lives—body, mind, and soul—thus, filling any areas that were left void by oppressing spirits with Jesus. You must always allow the Holy Spirit to be in control of your life.

How can you be continually filled by the Holy Spirit?

• Through praise, worship, and thanksgiving

...Be filled with the Spirit, speaking to one another in psalms and hymns and spiritual songs, singing and making melody in your heart to the Lord, giving thanks always for all things

to God the Father in the name of our Lord Jesus Christ.
EPHESIANS 5:18-20

These verses help us realize the importance of being grateful and to show it through hymns, songs, and praise. We should substitute our complaints and gossip with thanksgiving. Furthermore, we need to do it before, during, and after receiving our healing so that we could enjoy our healing miracle permanently, for praise and worship are a preventive medicine.

3. **By God's Word**

   ...He answered and said, 'It is written, 'Man shall not live by bread alone, but by every word that proceeds from the mouth of God.' **MATTHEW 4:4**

Another step required to keep your healing is to live and practice God's Word. You cannot live by your emotions; doing everything that simply "feels good" is the wrong way to live. Never allow your feelings or emotions to decide for you. Let us analyze the following three factors:

- Actions
- Faith
- Feelings

Concrete actions require faith, not feelings. After receiving your healing miracle, you might begin to experience the same symptoms as before; in this case, you must not make any decisions or take any action based on what you feel, but through faith resist the enemy! The Bible teaches that the devil tempted Jesus three times after the Holy Spirit came upon Him. You will most likely be tempted with greater intensity than before, after being filled with the Holy Spirit; the reason being that you are now moving in the supernatural realm and the enemy is doing everything in his power to make you fall.

Many people are unaware of the oppressing spirits operating in their lives until they are baptized with the Holy Spirit. This might sound strange, but it is nevertheless true. Demons tend to get very upset when the Holy Spirit is present. When Jesus dealt with Satan during His desert experience, He only used one weapon: God's Word. His Word is the sword of the Spirit or the anointing of the Holy Spirit's power. At each temptation Jesus answered: "It is written…" Similarly, after your baptism with the Holy Spirit, the next step you must take is to study God's Word (the Bible) with diligence and learn what it says. You need to live by God's Word and not by traditions, emotions, feelings, or circumstances.

4. **Put on the Armor of the Lord**

Put on the whole armor of God, that you may be able to stand against the wiles of the devil. **EPHESIANS 6:11**

Another step required to keep your healing is to wear the Armor of God. You must make the conscious decision to wear it every morning. During your prayer time, declare that you put on each piece until the complete armor is on; this is the best way to protect yourself from the plans and attacks of the enemy.

5. **Resist the enemy**

Therefore submit to God. Resist the devil and he will flee from you. **JAMES 4:7**

This verse clearly states that you must submit to God's Word to resist the devil; therefore, obey it and the people God has placed in your life to lead you. Why are we to resist? Because our minds are the enemy's battlefield; it is where he attacks in attempt to destroy us. Some people lose their healing when they begin to entertain sinful thoughts placed in their minds by the enemy. I say this so that, when you feel a symptom coming on, you don't say, "Oh no, I am not healed. I am still sick!" If you entertain these types of thoughts, instead of rebuking them, you lose your miracle. Therefore, learn to take captive every thought to the obedience of Jesus and refuse to allow any wicked thoughts, unbelief, rebelliousness, or anything else that may be trying to take over your thought life.

...Casting down arguments and every high thing that exalts itself against the knowledge of God, bringing every thought into captivity to the obedience of Christ... **2 CORINTHIANS 10:5**

Stop entertaining sinful thoughts; resist them with God's Word. Resist the enemy and he will flee from you. God has given you the power and authority to use His Word in His name. You are anointed by the Holy Spirit. When a sinful thought comes to your mind, just say, "I take captive every thought to the obedience of Jesus Christ. I declare myself healed, and I keep my healing in the name of Jesus. Amen!"

6. **Keep your good confession**

Let us hold fast the confession of our hope without wavering, for He who promised is faithful. **HEBREWS 10:23**

211

Jesus kept His good confession. Remember that He fought the good fight of faith and is the perfect example of someone who was able to keep the victory. Jesus knew He was the Son of God just as we know we are His children, by faith. Each decision Jesus made while on Earth was taken in faith. When He received the baptism with power (Luke 4:18), it was a declaration of faith. He lived in faith and knew how to receive it from His Father through the power of the Holy Spirit. He was tempted in every area of life, yet kept Himself holy by being completely obedient to the Father. He kept His good confession even when Pilate sentenced Him to death.

Jesus kept His Confession Even in His Darkest Hour

Pilate therefore said to Him, 'Are You a king then?' Jesus answered, 'You say rightly that I am a king. For this cause I was born, and for this cause I have come into the world, that I should bear witness to the truth. Everyone who is of the truth hears My voice.' **JOHN 18:37**

Jesus' disciples had abandoned Him. His hands were tied together and everything seemed a total loss, yet even under great suffering He managed to give His best answer, regardless of the fact that His answer (admitting that He was the Christ and King) would cause them to continue beating and torturing Him. When Pilate asked, His answer was firm and defiant. Sadly, the English and Spanish translations to His answer fail to relate its boldness; in the original language, it essentially says, "You can put your seal on it."

212

Upon His answer, I wouldn't doubt it if Saul, an overly zealous man of the Jewish tradition, was there to witness the judgment of one who claimed to be "the King of the Jews." In witnessing such a scene, something must have taken place in his heart. Saul may have hated hearing someone say He was "the King of the Jews," but the conviction in Jesus' confession must have impressed him deeply. I dare to say this because in the midst of His torture, Jesus firmly stated He was King. He could have easily stopped the torture by negating this important fact, and maybe would have even been spared the death at the cross. But He didn't. Instead, He kept His confession of God's Word that says that He is, indeed, our King.

Imagine Jesus' appearance at the time: beaten, spat on, bleeding, deeply wounded... Do you think He looked like a king? No, He sure didn't! He was having a very difficult time, worse than what we could ever imagine—and yet, after His first confession and suffering additional beatings and abuse, He declared it one more time: (paraphrased) "Yes, I am the Christ. You can put your seal on it!" At His weighty words, Pilate felt the conviction that Jesus was the King and therefore requested that the words, "King of the Jews," be written on His cross. Sadly, Pilate never had the nerve to stand on that truth.

Years later, while on his way to Damascus to continue his relentless persecution of the Church, Saul met Jesus face to face. Remembering the strength and conviction with which Jesus kept His confession, he finally believed and welcomed Jesus into his heart—he became a believer! At the end of his ministry, Saul tells his disciple Timothy:

Fight the good fight of faith, lay hold on eternal life, to which you were also called and have confessed the good confession in the presence of many witnesses. **1 TIMOTHY 6:12**

His words were as if saying, "I have experienced all that I have experienced because of that confession of faith. It touched me deeply and that is why I have fought the good fight, never giving up—the good fight of faith is fought until death". Now I say to you, let us ask God to forgive us for the times we have taken back our confession, especially during the heat of the battle. Instead, let us begin declaring that we are healed and affirm that we are free. Let us declare that the enemy does not have a foothold in our lives. Let us confess that even though our bodies are suffering with the symptoms of an illness, and even when the doctors say otherwise, God's Word is real, true, and powerful to overcome and defeat all sicknesses. One thing we cannot do is negate our confession. Jesus didn't.

Every terrible attack of the enemy can turn us into powerful warriors. The key is to maintain our confession. Let us meditate on the following: Contrary to what you may have learned, Jesus obtained His resurrection even before going to the cross, in the Garden of Gethsemane. There, in prayer, He fought the good fight of faith. Therefore, by the time He was arrested, He had already gained the title deed of His resurrection. Afterwards, when tempted to deny, He kept His good confession before Pontius Pilate. Likewise, let us imitate Him and learn to fight the good fight without complaining or bickering, and keep our good confession of faith. God has given everyone a measure of faith, and He will allow adverse situations to take place in our lives to help stretch our faith. Therefore, I say again:

Keep your confession strong and firm and you will retain your healing.

7. Continually walk in forgiveness

Now whom you forgive anything, I also forgive. For if indeed I have forgiven anything, I have forgiven that one for your sakes in the presence of Christ, lest Satan should take advantage of us; for we are not ignorant of his devices. 2 **CORINTHIANS 2:10, 11**

Another step required to keep your healing is to practice a lifestyle of forgiveness; this means that we must forgive all the time, not once in a while. Jesus said that offenses will always be a part of our lives and stumbling blocks will always appear in our path to make us fall, but He also said that we had to forgive at all times in order to keep the devil at a disadvantage and away from us.

Testimony: A woman suffered a car accident that destroyed the ligaments in her right knee and damaged some nerves. She was close to spending the rest of her life in a wheelchair when she decided to visit our church. After we prayed and ministered to her, particularly in the area of unforgiveness, she decided to forgive everyone who had hurt her. Immediately after, the Lord healed her. Today, she rejoices as she dances and sings to the Lord, giving Him all the praise and glory.

8. Keep the right relationships

Adulterers and adulteresses! Do you not know that friendship with the world is enmity with God? Whoever therefore wants to be a friend of the world makes himself an enemy of God. JAMES 4:4

We know the relationships we engage in can powerfully affect our behavior in either a positive or negative way. If our friends exhibit negative behaviors, we must quickly end those relationships. Likewise, we must stop visiting places that can affect our good judgment and lead us to sin. Choosing to befriend the world leads us to making God our enemy—the Scriptures clearly state that a friend to the world is an enemy of God. I know of people who were healed, but later allowed the enemy to entice them back into the world, causing them to lose their healing. Many of them lost their lives due to their choice of befriending the world through maintaining the wrong relationships.

9. Develop a lifestyle of prayer

...Praying always with all prayer and supplication in the Spirit, being watchful to this end with all perseverance and supplication for all the saints... EPHESIANS 6:18

God's Word teaches that we must pray to the Father, everyday. This is really an important key to maintaining our healing. We must continually go before the Father and simply talk to Him, knowing that we are His children and that He loves us dearly. Then we can receive from Him the entirety of His blessings. Remember to keep a rigorous and continuous prayer life!

10. Crucify the flesh everyday

Then He said to them all, 'If anyone desires to come after Me, let him deny himself, and take up his cross daily, and follow Me.' LUKE 9:23

What is the flesh? The flesh is our ego which must be crucified daily. Jesus said we must deny ourselves, meaning we must deny our wants, our way of seeing things, and the way we feel in order to do what God wants, feels, and thinks. When we seek to satisfy our personal agendas and will, we become fertile ground to the enemy's continuous attacks; thus, becoming vulnerable to sickness and oppression.

11. Fellowship in a church, House of Peace (small group), or a discipleship

...Not forsaking the assembling of ourselves together, as is the manner of some, but exhorting one another, and so much the more as you see the Day approaching. **HEBREWS 10:25**

Finally, we retain our healing by strengthening our spirit as we fellowship with our brothers and sisters at church, a cell group, or a discipleship. The main purpose for fellowship is to praise God together, but also to give God the opportunity to bless us, to assure and affirm us, to encourage and strengthen us so that we can resist the devil's attacks.

Review

The most common causes of losing one's healing are: Receiving it by the faith of others, giving the devil a foothold, lacking the biblical foundation to defend it, having a negative confession, and continuing to live in sin. Sometimes, however, it is simply a mystery which God will reveal to us some day. Furthermore, there are also 11 steps you must keep in mind to keep your healing:

- Make Jesus the Lord of every area of your life because, if the void left by the sickness is not filled with His presence, the spirit of sickness can return and take over that area again; this latter condition can be worse than the former.

- Seek to be continuously filled with the Holy Spirit, with the evidence of speaking in other tongues; this can only be done through praise and worship.

- Live by God's Word, not by your emotions or feelings.

- Put on the Armor of the Lord every day.

- Resist the enemy; otherwise, he will attack your mind causing you to doubt and eventually lose your healing.

- Keep your good confession and learn to fight the good fight of faith, like Jesus (and later Paul) did when He went before Ponce Pilate; do this regardless of what it might cost you.

- Practice a lifestyle of forgiveness, because bitterness is an open door to the enemy, and it gives him the legal right to attack and oppress you.

- Establish good relationships with the right people; those who confess God's Word and who will never influence you to abandon the good fight of faith.

- Live a lifestyle of prayer. Enough said.

- Crucify your flesh, daily. Remember that your flesh is your ego or your desire to live independently from God. Learn to deny yourself; this basically means to renounce to your personal desires, thoughts, and feelings in order to do what God wants, desires, and thinks. In doing so you will discover His will for you, which is the best that can ever happen to you.

■ Fellowship in the church, Houses of Peace (small groups that meet in a house), and in your discipleship so that, through your worship, God can strengthen your faith and bless you.

In conclusion, these things must be done in order to keep your healing; otherwise, it will be impossible to do it in your own strength. The only control you have over any situation is your choice to live a pure and holy life before God; to close every door to the enemy, and to refuse to give him a foothold that will give him the legal right to attack you. You must learn to depend on God's supernatural grace, which will give you the strength needed to resist the devil and to take every thought captive to the obedience of Christ—He is the only One who can give you the strength to overcome every temptation or symptom. His supernatural grace upon you will strengthen and keep you firm in your conviction and confession; so you may speak life and not death; declare that you will live and not die.

You must make the faith-filled declaration that *Jesus is Lord* and that He took your place on the cross. He took your sickness and your pain; this is God's plan of redemption for your healing. Jesus paid the wages of your sin at the cross. Everything has been provided and paid for God's children. You and I may not deserve it, and we certainly could never have paid our debt, but we can receive it anyways through our faith in Christ Jesus. This is the only way we are delivered and set free to live in divine health.

Many believe that receiving a healing miracle is the best God has to offer; although this is certainly a good and wonderful thing, the best of God in regard to healing is to live in divine health. The steps mentioned help us to maintain our healing and live in divine health from the top of our head to the sole of our feet. This is the reason it becomes necessary to declare God's Word to our bodies— the temple of the Holy Spirit— every day. I wake up every morning and declare that the Holy Spirit vivifies my body and that I have a long and abundant life. I have so much life in me through the power of the resurrection, that this makes my body come alive, allowing my cells to be renewed and stay healthy, and forbidding any sickness to invade my body. This can be true for you too. Therefore, begin to cast out every spirit of infirmity and resist the devil. Remember that the devil was defeated at the Cross of Calvary. Keep your good confession of faith and begin declaring what God did to enjoy living in good health. Now that you are healed, share it with others. Pray for the sick and impart the healing that you received. In my next book, you will learn how to heal others by the power that resides in the name of Jesus.

Prayer for healing

Heavenly Father, in the name of Jesus, I pray for everyone reading this book and who is now suffering with an illness. In the name of Jesus, I declare the Word of God over their lives; thus, bringing upon them God's faith, and I decree the words found in 1 Peter 2:24 that say, "By His stripes you were healed." In the name of Jesus, I close every door to Satan and remind him that he was defeated at the cross. Now, be healed in the name of Jesus.

If you are sick, now is the time for you to take ownership of the divine inheritance that is rightfully yours as a child of God and co-heir with Jesus Christ. Today, begin declaring your healing and God's Word, live a holy life apart from sin, forgive others, and submit to God. In other words, put your faith in action.

Note:

To pray with Apostle Guillermo Maldonado and receive his powerful impartation, visit: kingjesus.org/jesus-heals-prayer

BIBLIOGRAPHY

Blue Letter Bible. "Dictionary and Word Search for rhçma (Strong's 4487)". 1996-2009. 1 Sep 2009. <http://www.blueletterbible.org/lang/lexicon/lexicon.cfm?Strongs=G4487&t=KJV >

Expanded Edition the Amplified Bible. Zondervan Bible Publishers, 1987 – Lockman Foundation, USA. ISBN: 0 31095168 2

Real Academia Española, Diccionario de la Lengua Española, http://www.rae.es/.

Reina-Valera 1960, Copyright © 1960 Sociedades Bíblicas en América Latina; Copyright © renovado 1988, Sociedades Bíblicas Unidas.

Strong, James. LL.D, S.T.D. Nueva Concordancia Strong Exhaustiva. Nashville, TN–Miami, FL: Editorial Caribe, Inc./División Thomas Nelson Publishers, 2002. ISBN: 0-89922-382-6.

Osborn, T.L., Healing the Sick, ed. Harrison House Inc., Tulsa Oklahoma, 1992.

The Tormont Webster's Illustrated Encyclopedic Dictionary. ©1990 Tormont Publications.

Vine, W.E. Vine: diccionario expositivo de palabras del antiguo testamento y del nuevo testamento exhaustivo. Nashville, TN: Editorial Caribe, Inc./División de Thomas Nelson, Inc., 1999. ISBN: 0 89922 495 4.

Ward, Lock A. Nuevo Diccionario de la Biblia. Editorial Unilit: Miami, Florida, 1999. ISBN: 0 7899-0217-6

Holy Bible, NIV. 1973, 1978, 1984 International Bible Society.

To pray with Apostle Guillermo Maldonado and
receive his powerful impartation, visit:
kingjesus.org/jesus-heals-prayer